TESTIMONA

Leaders Who Ask: Building Fearless Cultures by telling less and asking more

Deep within everyone is unbounded potential and the role of the leader is to draw this out. This is not achieved through instructing or telling but through suspending judgement, asking questions and listening intently. This book provides a powerful approach for leaders to build culture by assisting one human being at a time to transform their life. This is truly the great honour of leadership.

Dr David Cooke, Managing Director - Konica Minolta Business Solutions Australia

Corrinne has helped me realise the value of embracing a less directive leadership approach. If you want to ask more and tell less, this book sets out how in an engaging way.

Simone Zelencich, Executive Director, People & Culture - The Royal Children's Hospital

Leaders today need the critical balance between business and people acumen. They are expected to have a range of tools to increase business performance as well as develop the critical soft skills needed for setting a culture that focuses on people and stimulates innovation.

I recommend this book to leaders who strive to set a high performing culture by motivating and empowering all within their organisation, thus enhancing leadership, organisational performance and staff retention.

Matthew Jackson, Chief Executive Officer, Parks Victoria

Incorporating aspects of coaching into your leadership practice can leverage some strong results in individual and collective team engagement and performance over time. Corinne's book provides a framework to work within and great tips to try. This isn't a quick fix, rather an opportunity to reflect on your leadership impact and question whether there are improvements you can make. After all, we are only as successful as the teams and culture that we build and enable.

Bridgid Connors, Chief Human Resources Officer - Monash University

A large proportion of leaders I meet in the service sector think they need to have all the answers. This limiting belief exists because they have not yet realised the power of questions.

When I witness great leaders ask staff rather than tell, the result is a highly engaged workforce, and an engaged workforce is a precursor to quality customer service. The questioning techniques this book presents are practical and highly effective for developing staff in the workplace. It will be a valuable resource for me to introduce to organisations that are determined to create consistent quality service cultures.

Jaquie Scammell, Australia's Leading Customer Relations Expert, author of *Creating a Customer Service Mindset*

Corrinne has the ability to create a mindful and highly effective leader in all of us through her gift of making complex things simple.

The 'coach as leader' techniques explored by Corrinne have connectivity to collaborative and innovative cultures that bring energy and engagement to our organisations, similar to the way Corrinne herself brings energy and clarity to your leadership team.

Always reflective in her style, Corrinne will make you examine yourself. The book is a capacity building journey that creates a greater depth of personal awareness through better understanding your own leadership style and preferences, forcing you to be overt in your intentions.

It provides the practical tools to do what I love the most: build a culture of innovation and curiosity—a productive and engaged sweet spot.

Sarah Cumming, Managing Director - Gippsland Water

Leaders Who Ask

Leaders Who

Ask

Building
Fearless Cultures
by **telling less**
and **asking more**

CORRINNE ARMOUR

Published by Bacca House Press

BHP

Bacca House Press

ISBN: 978-0-6482812-1-4

A catalogue record for this book is available from the National Library of Australia

CONTENTS

PREFACE

Warning

Reading this book will do nothing for your leadership capability, nor the engagement and productivity of your team. Just as buying a fabulous new set of power tools from Bunnings won't make you a handyman, reading this book won't make you a better leader.

To become a better leader, you need to **do something** with what you read.

Are you ready to build a Fearless Culture? Are you willing to hold back what you know and ask your people what they know? Do you have the courage and commitment needed?

No? Then find another book.

Yes? Then welcome. I am delighted to lead you on this journey.

My wish for you is threefold:

1. that you develop a set of competencies that are valuable to a leader

2. that you are able to employ them to build the capability of individuals, teams and whole organisations through formal, structured conversations, informal corridor conversations, and by conducting effective and engaging meetings

3. that you discover the power of asking more and telling less to build Fearless Cultures.

The first working title for this book was called 'The Lazy Leader'. It was a tongue in cheek title—the *leader who asks* is not lazy. Yet once established they might appear to be lazy because leadership seems almost effortless for them.

No longer jumping in with the answers, they have the courage to let go of the need to control. Armed with coaching skills, they build rapport quickly, listen deeply and their questions engage others. While they always seem to have a purpose, they also have a sense of creativity about them and a belief that outcomes will be achieved. They run great meetings without appearing to put effort into either the planning or the chairing. You can see them in the corridors engaging in animated conversation. And when you walk through the open plan office, there's a buzz of energy and productivity.

A vision of the Pied Piper comes to mind ... that's the *leader who asks.*

ACKNOWLEDGEMENTS

Being allowed into the hearts and minds of leaders is an honour and privilege. To all the leaders and leadership teams I have worked with over the last fifteen years, thank you for the trust you have placed in me, and for the great work you are doing. A special thank you to those whose stories I have shared in the pages of this book.

Gratitude to my family: my parents, Ian and Helene, who were my first coaches, my sister Fleur, who always supports me, and Min Thein, Jessi and Maithy who are now perhaps my greatest teachers.

My first two books were co-authored with Anneli Blundell and Belinda Cohen. Whenever I became stuck writing this book, I have channelled their wisdom and encouragement.

Thanks to my support team who keep me facing the right direction every day: Sheryl, Gladys and Melinda. And to my wonderful editor, Joanna Yardley.

My constant inspiration for doing more and being more comes from the Thought Leaders community. Thank you to everyone who helps me to constantly lift my standards and the impact of my work, especially Matt Church and Peter Cook.

And finally, thank you to you—the reader. You are a leader who cares enough about your impact to want to become *a leader who asks*. The world needs you.

This book is dedicated to all leaders who know that leadership is the answer and that they are part of both the problem and the solution.

The *Leader Who Asks:* My story

Many years ago, I was leading a cross-functional project team of 70+ people. At short notice, I was asked to participate in the pilot of an internal training program, and then provide feedback before the program went live across the organisation. Being a bit of a learning junkie, I said yes without knowing what the program was really about. Turns out it was 'Leader as Coach' at a time when 'coaching' was not known or understood in the corporate world.

That day blew my mind, and I left energised and inspired. I had shifted from not knowing that coaching even existed outside a sporting context, to understanding that a coaching approach was the way I naturally led. Prior to that workshop, I was already aware that my leadership style was a little different from many around me: I preferred to ask questions and guide learning rather than give answers—tell less, ask more. (I have always been comfortable, as a leader, not having all the answers.)

I had sometimes wondered if I were a bit 'lazy', not really a leader at all. But that day, I discovered that my leadership style was valid. And I gained ways of codifying coaching skills and extending my competency with new tricks and tools. I felt empowered and ready to step up and use my shiny new coaching skills.

That first coaching skills program did two things for me. First, it validated (and extended) my natural leadership style.

Second, it set me on a career path that focused more on coaching, and led me to where I am now—a leadership expert who helps others develop Fearless Leadership and build Fearless Cultures

Chapter 1

What's happening?

 *Craig sighed deeply, clearly shaken. The staff engagement results had blindsided him. He was surprised at the lack of positive movement since last year, despite the focused efforts from him and the whole executive team.*

After last year's survey, the CEO made engagement a priority across the organisation. Focus groups were conducted to understand the sentiments and the issues; project teams were put in place; and a number of initiatives were successfully implemented. A complete refresh of the organisation's values had begun.

Craig had also focused on making changes to his own behaviour as a leader, and he had been looking forward to seeing what impacts that had on his division's engagement results.

The results were just as bad as last year. It seemed that people hadn't taken any notice of the good work that had been done. Sure, it takes a long time to make an impact on an organisation of this size and the external climate had been challenging with two key competitors taking significant market share over the last year, but what more could he do?

Craig's leadership style had served him well until now, and he wasn't sure what he was missing. There was so much that needed to be done, and it wasn't as if he had any spare time. He dropped the report back onto his desk and stared out the window. Maybe it was time for a different approach?

Craig's story is soul destroying, isn't it? As I move between a diverse range of organisations across multiple sectors, I see dedicated and committed leaders working hard (perhaps too hard). Despite their good intentions and their best efforts, they are struggling to achieve their own potential and are unable to unlock the potential of their teams. This constrains organisational culture and impacts the bottom line. That's a lot of wasted effort.

Is there untapped potential across your organisation? Are you building engaged and productive teams? Or are you stuck in expert mode, solving all the problems yourself, rather than empowering and developing your teams and building a Fearless Culture?

Leadership matters. We know it matters inside the organisation because we have all experienced good and bad leadership. Leadership matters externally too. When stock market analysts are valuing public companies, part of what they are looking at is the quality of leadership in the organisation. A study by Deloitte calculated a leadership premium of up to 15.7%.[1] This means that when you are under good leadership, there is a boost to your share price of almost 16%. And of course the opposite is also true: there's a 16% hit on your share price for poor leadership.

Why is it happening?

Being a leader feels like hard work

As leaders, we feel we are constantly telling people what to do. It seems there is never a time when someone is not waiting for us to solve a problem or provide an instruction on what's next. It's tiring; it keeps us stuck in the day to day and prevents us from doing anything strategic. The weight of leading a team—whether it's 10 people or 10,000—can be heavy.

Sometimes we feel the responsibility of having to 'know' everything and as leaders, we can get anxious if we don't have all the answers.

Our ability to communicate with and engage our team directly impacts its success. The team meeting is a common way to meet this need. But **many leaders struggle to run an effective meeting**, creating instead a monologue better suited to inducing sleep than building shared purpose.

And then there are those crucial performance conversations— the ones we put off. We stew on what to say, how to say it, and how the team will respond. Perhaps there are **people in your team who need some extra support**. Providing development feedback can be hard and thankless work, especially when there is no shift in behaviour or outcomes.

All this can translate into sleepless nights.

What if there was a way to empower your people to solve problems themselves? What if you didn't need all the answers? Would you like a way to prepare less for meetings, and yet have more engaging conversations and better outcomes? How would it be to feel more confident in performance conversations?

Staff engagement is patchy

Maybe your organisation is growing rapidly, and that's exciting, right? You are all doing great work, and the customer values what you are delivering. But with growth comes risk and signs of organisational growing pains are showing. Old ways of communicating are not working so well, and with greater size and complexity it's becoming harder to keep messages consistent.

Maybe your organisation isn't growing; it's been around for a while and the legacy of history is slowing things down. The annual engagement survey shows that staff engagement scores are still low, despite the actions to address this. (And you didn't need a survey to tell you that anyway, did you?) Not matter what you try, it's hard to make a real connection with your team. While it's easy to give direction, providing inspiration is so much harder. People seem stuck and lacking in purpose.

Problems may be simmering under the surface, and it's hard to identify the real issues. You may not have the confidence to surface tensions, or you lack the framework to respond. When challenges arise, you find yourself fighting fires rather than proactively building team culture.

It's important to retain what is great about your organisational culture and leadership style. How about embracing additional ways of communicating, operating and leading?

Leadership bench-strength is lacking

In a 2013 Australian Employee Engagement Survey, 38% of the 2,223 professionals who responded did not agree with the statement 'my manager helps me perform at my best'.[2] There's something wrong with this picture, and I don't think it's changed much in the few years since.

A key responsibility of leadership is developing others, and yet **it's challenging to grow our people.** While we might have the right intentions, we get busy and performance conversations don't happen outside the annual performance review process. (And even then, most of the conversations are simply to tick the box.)

Or perhaps you do prioritise regular feedback discussions, but they don't seem to have much impact. Conversations on the job—where you know it counts—get awkward and opportunities are missed. Staff members are not progressing as you would like, and despite your focus, they complain there's no investment in their development.

When people feel undervalued, undeveloped, and disconnected from organisational purpose, they may let you know by leaving. Is it time to bring some new tools into your leadership toolkit?

The results aren't there

Team performance across the organisation is inconsistent with some teams not delivering on expectations, and there is a lack of individual and team accountability. You might be thinking the lack of ability to hit team KPIs is because of the quality of people in the team. Other teams in the company work well, and yet you seem unable to turn this around.

In many organisations, especially where there is a strong professional expertise (such as hospitals, law firms, engineering practices), GMs have reached the level they are at through **excellent technical skills** and willingness to work hard.

Perhaps that's you.

But now you are struggling to engage. You are working too hard, trying to control processes and people, and still not getting results.

Your primary expertise in (say) medicine does not automatically give you a secondary expertise in leadership. You may need help to build leadership capabilities to engage, empower, and develop your people. Like asking more and telling less.

Let's empower leaders to be brave enough and skilled enough to connect deeply, lead fearlessly and achieve results that transform.

You see that more is possible

Perhaps your team is performing really well: there's a healthy team dynamic, strong relationships within the team and with stakeholders, a culture of giving and receiving feedback, and performance targets are being met. Unlike Craig, who we meet at the beginning on the book, your engagement scores are high.

Yet you believe that more is possible.

There is a better way

If you are looking for a way to step up as a leader and continually grow your team so that the whole team steps up too, this book will help you.

Let's empower leaders to be brave enough and skilled enough to connect deeply, lead fearlessly and achieve results that transform. Let's build leadership. Let's create Fearless Cultures.

What is a Fearless Culture?

Fearless Cultures get results. The performance bar is constantly being lifted through timely conversations that promote curiosity and lead to individual and team development. The things that matter are surfaced and resolved.

When groups of people come together, the conversation is focused, lively and creative. Innovation is an approach to everyday activity—creating and harnessing insight—and not just a concept that's peddled around the organisation. People at all levels feel empowered in their roles. They feel they are being invested in, and supported and cared for. This environment promotes the kind of positive risk taking that comes from safety to challenge, to try things out and to fail.

Fearless Cultures have a buzz about them, and you don't need to see the staff survey results to know that engagement is high. Accountability is in action every day: personal accountability, team accountability, and the willingness to hold one another accountable.

In Fearless Cultures, leaders tell less and ask more.

Chapter 2

The *Leader Who Asks Ladder* to a Fearless Culture

Asking more and telling less is hard to achieve. Building a Fearless Culture doesn't happen overnight. In fact, it doesn't happen very often, and when it does, it's the result of the cumulative focus of the leaders across the organisation.

Before we start, let's be very clear: we are talking about the leader's **coaching focus** and **skill**, not their technical skill. You, and most of your leaders, will be highly competent in your technical skill set. Your technical skill set was probably a major contribution to promotion to a leadership role but it is unlikely to be a key factor in success at the leadership level.

A leader's primary skill set might be accounting, nursing, design or law, and for each the secondary skill set is leadership. This book focuses on the secondary skill set; it explores the leader's skill in the nuances of connecting with, engaging, and developing their team members.

As a leader, your success comes from the team's success, and not your own; it's your **leadership** expertise that matters. A key way to access and accelerate the success of the team is through becoming a *leader who asks* and embracing a coaching approach.

Let's have a look at leaders through the lens of their coaching focus. Imagine a ladder, and like most ladders, we begin at the bottom.

	CULTURE	LEADER	LEADER'S ASK vs TELL FOCUS	Team Productivity
	Fearless	Fearless	SKILLFUL	x 5
	Engaged	Committed	CONSISTENT	x 3
	Connected	Present	INCONSISTENT	x 2
	Functioning	Distracted	AWARE	x 1
	Disengaged	Indifferent	DISSENTING	x -2

Increasing return (top arrow) / *Increasing cost* (bottom arrow)

Figure 1: *The Leader Who Asks Ladder*

The Indifferent Leader

The **Indifferent** Leader (and really I am using the term 'leader' here for consistency, and not because this group has earned it) does not engage in a coaching focus at all. They may be completely unaware of the possibility, or they may be **DISSENTING** from a coaching focus. Full stop!

This leader may never have had the opportunity to experience or learn a coaching approach, or it could be something they have heard of but with which they disagree. *'It's quicker and more effective to tell people what to do. After all, we pay them to do a job, don't we?'* The culture of this team is **Disengaged**, and not surprisingly team productivity is low, probably at cost to the business.

Meet Jessica, the Indifferent Leader

Quick witted, a strong strategic thinker, technically gifted, and highly ambitious, Jessica attained her first senior leadership position in her early 30s. Those close to her thought she had the ability to reach CEO level, and yet few believed she would. A recent staff survey indicated that Jessica's team was disengaged, with most staff believing that Jessica cared little about them, nor that she was willing to invest personally in their development. Her executive colleagues experienced her as competitive, untrusting and needing to be in control.

For her part, Jessica was frustrated with the stagnating skill level of her team, its lack of willingness to take accountability for individual and team results, and its reluctance to put in any discretionary effort. She worked long hours to achieve good results, and she could not understand why her team was not willing to do the same.

As an Indifferent Leader, Jessica's primary leadership style was directive and impersonal. People in her team were unsure of how they could improve because their performance was never assessed or developed.

Her career success to date resulted from ambition and hard work, a high IQ and an almost Machiavellian approach to leadership. It wasn't that she was deliberately controlling and disempowering, Jessica simply didn't appreciate the importance of connecting with people and the value of a coaching approach overlaid on her existing leadership style.

Indifferent Leaders are dissenting towards a coaching approach. They may:

- be very competent technically
- have a strong and inflexible leadership style that does not include coaching
- focus on commanding rather than building rapport
- deliberately disregard the need for asking, instead telling their people what to do
- have a weak leadership style and weak technical skills
- have a low care for people, or a lack of ability to express the care they have
- be a new leader and are learning the ropes of leadership
- or they may be like Jessica—simply unaware of the alternatives.

Whatever the 'cause', this leader is indifferent to the value of coaching skills and their team is likely to be unproductive and disengaged. Absenteeism could be a problem in this team. Or worse, 'presenteeism', where people have checked out and yet still come to work each day.

Indifferent Leaders are a big risk to organisational culture. The Dale Carnegie Institute estimates that 'reactions to him or her explain 84% of how employees feel about their organization'.[3]

The Distracted Leader

Next up the ladder, we have the **Distracted** Leader. This leader is **AWARE** of a coaching approach but has yet to embrace it. They typically know more is possible from their leadership and are beginning to look for ways to make that happen.

Distracted Leaders work hard, yet they are not rewarded with the results they might like or expect. *'I have tried everything to get my people engaged, and nothing works. I am starting to wonder if it's me.'* This wondering might keep them awake at night.

Meet Jordan, the Distracted Leader

Jordan is the CEO of an aged care provider. He is committed to his team, the residents, the families they support, and to the sector as a whole. His passion fired his long working week, and yet he is exhausted.

Jordan felt like everyone relied on him. He had tried various strategies to get his executive team to take greater ownership and step up, and yet still found himself the 'go to' person for solving problems across the organisation. Others were reluctant to make decisions without endorsement from the CEO.

Jordan was stretched and recognised the need to reduce his operational focus so he had the headspace to focus on the strategic issues of organisational growth in a sector undergoing significant change.

He was looking for help, which he thought would come in the form of training and support for his executive team. He also had sufficient self-awareness to begin questioning how his own leadership style could be contributing to the challenges he faced.

Jordan's realisation that his own leadership style was limiting his executive team was a confronting one. His efforts to be supportive were seen as micromanagement. His drive to provide the answers was limiting his team's ability to make mistakes and learn. Worse still, Jordan's behaviour was being modelled by the executives, with a flow on effect of micromanagement through the organisation.

Aware leaders are distracted in their coaching focus and may:

- be very competent technically
- be aware of some coaching skills and are either not confident to use them, or not convinced of the value of applying them
- be observing other leaders building productive and engaged teams, and wondering what their secret is
- be aware that their current approach is not working and be seeking alternatives.

Their team will be **Functioning**—certainly not disengaged yet not engaged either. This is a lost opportunity for increasing productivity and developing organisational culture.

The Present Leader

The **Present** Leader has taken on the challenge and opportunity of a coaching approach, yet is **INCONSISTENT** in its application. This leader is encouraged by the hard measure of increased team productivity and the soft measure of a greater feeling of connection among team members. They invest in building rapport, strengthening relationships, asking questions that lead to insight, and providing real-time feedback that builds skill and confidence.

Then deadlines loom or a team member is on leave so the pressure increases and the coaching approach is dropped in favour of a directive style. *'I like the coaching approach, and know it is working, but I don't have time for it right now.'* Curt instructions are given, and feedback opportunities are missed. Team members, while still feeling connected, are unsure of what to expect from an inconsistent approach to leadership.

Meet Lola, the Present Leader

On the executive team, Lola has embraced coaching skills to support her approach to leadership. She is conscious of 'asking' rather than 'telling' when her managers come to her with problems, and her intention is to empower her people. She has always been committed to the concept of continual development and now, with a coaching approach, she has found a way to support this.

Lola recently told me that 'I am getting some of the best results I have ever got. And I feel as if I am working less. I am just having coaching conversations.' Lola is well on her way to becoming a coaching leader.

Feedback from her team indicates that Lola's coaching approach is still inconsistently applied. She moves unpredictably between leadership styles and her team doesn't know what version of Lola will show up. This is not surprising as Lola builds new habits to balance a more directive approach to leadership.

With continued focus, Lola will certainly move up the Leader Who Asks Ladder.

The Present Leader has coaching skills in their leadership toolkit and draws on these skills often and yet still inconsistently. They are beginning to see the benefit of a coaching approach on team culture and on productivity. Team members are likely to feel more **Connected** to this leader, and their development needs are considered important; however, the inconsistency of the leader's style will impact team productivity and morale.

The Present Leader may also be erring on the side of too much coaching by taking a coaching approach when other tools from their leadership toolkit would be more appropriate.

There is a tipping point here, where the conscious and competent application of coaching skills create a breakthrough in culture and productivity. This is the invisible line that once crossed can't be seen but can be felt by everyone—the line of decreasing cost and increasing return.

The Committed Leader

The **Committed Leader** is **CONSISTENT** in their application of coaching skills. The committed leader's aspirational goal is to develop productive teams and engaged cultures.

Meet Paul, the Committed Leader

Paul, a GM, describes his earlier leadership style as 'Fix-it man'. His sense of identity came from being able to solve problems and sort out issues for people. Prompted by feedback he was getting from his team, including terms like 'micromanager', 'highly opinionated' and 'controlling', Paul engaged a leadership expert who encouraged and supported him to adopt a coaching approach.

Now (some years later), Paul's style is 'listen, coach and influence. Assist my direct reports to come to conclusions themselves.' Coaching skills are near the top of his leadership toolkit.

Of course, there are times when he directs, times when he mentors, and times when he applies other leadership styles. Mostly though, he coaches in a formal sense through career development conversations and performance reviews, or simply informal corridor conversations on his way around the organisation.

Paul has developed a library of questions that prompt his managers' thinking and leads them to their own insights. This builds his direct reports' confidence that they are capable and are growing as leaders.

Engagement scores are high across Paul's teams, with excellent productivity measures to match.

It's important to note that Paul hasn't always led in this way. In the first year in this role, he struggled to connect with some of the managers who report to him; he was often stressed and felt a great need to know all the answers. His development to a leader who asks has been deliberately and progressively achieved.

The Committed Leader embraces coaching skills and makes them their own, adapting to what's needed by the people, the situation and the task. This leader makes judgments in the moment and applies coaching principles to their leadership to build **Engaged** and productive teams.

The way the Fearless
Leader shows up
optimises the potential
of individuals in
the team, and of
the team itself.

The Fearless Leader

At the top of the *Leader Who Asks Ladder*, we have **Fearless Leaders** who may be highly skilled in their primary expertise (marketing, engineering, IT etc.), and who are **Skilful** in applying a coaching focus.

The way the Fearless Leader shows up—their presence as well as the approach they take—optimises the potential of individuals in the team, and of the team itself. Their leadership builds highly productive teams and creates Fearless Cultures.

Fearless Leaders build Fearless Cultures. In Fearless Cultures, there are high levels of **engagement** across all levels (as contrasted to the average Australian workplace where engagement is around 24%).[4] With higher engagement comes better workplace relations, reduced sick leave, greater discretionary effort—the list goes on .... In Fearless Cultures, people and teams take **accountability** for their behaviour, their work and their results. Fearless Cultures are productive cultures where people want to belong.

Their ability to draw out the wisdom from others means they lead dynamic and challenging meetings. People who work with these leaders feel they are being invested in. Their clients enjoy working with them because they learn something beyond the agreed transaction.

Fearless Leaders have the courage to connect deeply, lead fearlessly, and they (and their teams) achieve results.

Meet Frank, the Fearless Leader

Working in an international finance organisation, Frank is the type of leader who instils confidence in others, up and down the chain of command. He is often brought in to turn around an operational division or bring a major project back on track. While he is very results driven, his coaching approach raises the performance of people— individuals and teams—beyond what even they think is possible.

Frank is focused and calm. He is aware there are multiple ways to attain success. He knows that good people are often their own harshest critic and helping people uncover their own learning is far more powerful than allocating blame and judgment.

He is confident and steadfast as a leader, and at the same time will admit he doesn't have the answers and can show vulnerability.

Frank asks the kind of questions that keep you thinking way after the conversation has ended. One of Frank's special skills is silence; he asks a question and waits patiently while you gather your thoughts (and sometimes muster up courage to voice what you are thinking) and respond. He never fills the space, waiting instead for others to take up the invitation.

Frank knows his key role, as a leader, is to develop others. His presence and approach bring out the best in people and teams, and he builds Fearless Cultures along the way.

'Before you are a leader, success is all about growing yourself. When you become a leader, success is all about growing others' —Jack Welch (former Chairman and CEO of GE). The Fearless Leader knows this. Technical skills are the ticket to play, not the road to success. Coaching competencies help the Fearless Leader achieve success through growing others.

Where are *you* on the *Leader Who Asks Ladder*?

Now that I have briefly explained each level of the *Leader Who Asks Ladder*, what are you thinking about your own leadership style? What's come up for you?

Where are you now on the ladder? Which level do you want to reach, and what would that give you? What benefits would it bring to your team? How would that advance the purpose of your organisation?

Chapter 3

The *Leader Who Asks*: What it is and what it isn't

Building a Fearless Culture

Organisations that have developed a 'coaching culture'—where the majority of people in the organisation use questioning techniques and coaching principles rather than telling people what to do—develop Fearless Cultures.

There are good reasons for investing in developing such a culture. Organisations that implement a coaching culture report these benefits[5]:

- Engagement: Increased engagement with people means they are more inspired to make decisions themselves.

- Improvement focus: People initiated continuous improvement projects, process improvements and fun events.

- Productivity: Increased productivity, decreased absenteeism and other non-scheduled work absences.

- Collaboration: Better feeling of work teams and increased collaboration within and across business units.

- Increased performance: Measured by key performance indicators.

Becoming a *leader who asks* is not about becoming a coach. This book is **not** about teaching you to be a coach. There are other books—and some great programs—that will do that.

This is about adding coaching skills and qualities to complement and extend your existing leadership style. The simplest and most profound way to do this is to engage others through questions, rather than defaulting to a quick fix by providing an answer.

In the late 90s and early 2000s, 'Leader as Coach' programs were popular in the corporate world. The basic proposition of most of these programs was that:

- Coaches develop people effectively.

- Leaders need to develop people effectively.

- (Therefore) all leaders should be coaches (all the time).

This was not a smart idea, any more than it would be a smart idea to insist that all our leaders adopt a command and control leadership style. Turning all our leaders into coaches is:

- **Unrealistic**: Coaching is a professional discipline. Learning to be a coach takes extensive training, supervision and experience over long periods. With the leadership development budget available to most leaders in corporate Australia, this level of investment and attainment is unavailable.

- **Unwise**: Coaching is **one** leadership and development intervention. Insisting that leaders coach during every interaction is about as smart as inviting a chef to use a vegetable paring knife to cut all her ingredients. The best leaders are those with flexible leadership styles, and those who are able to adopt a situational approach.

In this book, we talk about complementing a leader's skills and not overwriting them. To build Fearless Cultures, leaders need to add coaching skills to their existing leadership toolkits. They must make conscious choices about when to use elements of coaching skills right across their current leadership style.

So what is coaching?

When I work with leaders, there is usually a lack of understanding as to what coaching actually is, and how it is different from mentoring or other forms of development available to a leader. So before we go too far, let's get clear on what we mean by coaching in the context of building a Fearless Culture. We'll start by looking at what coaching is not.

Mentoring

Typically, a mentor has expertise in their field, and transfers knowledge, skills and experience to a less experienced practitioner. The mentor is 'older and wiser', either literally or metaphorically.

A leader acts as a mentor when they 'tell' a member of their team how to do something based on their experience.

Sandy is an experienced project director who is highly skilled in the technical elements of project management. Her emotional intelligence and good people skills have resulted in a strong reputation across the organisation for being an effective influencer.

Steven is a young project manager operating in another part of the company leading his first big stand-alone project. He has had trouble relating to the project steering committee and has been unable to get committee members aligned on key project objectives.

Sandy is mentoring Steven on the best methodologies for stakeholder engagement, how to run effective steering committee meetings, and ways to influence senior leaders without being seen to be telling them what to do. Their conversations typically involve Steven outlining his current challenges, and Sandy sharing past situations where she has had similar challenges and how she addressed them. Steven finds these meetings invaluable and leaves with new techniques to try out immediately.

Training

A trainer teaches a person, or typically a group, how to do something. This could be a formal classroom session, or informal, on-job training. Leaders tend to train more often in junior leadership roles where they are showing people how to use predefined processes or approaches.

A leader acts as a trainer when they train operational staff on how to use a particular system, or when they teach someone how the company approaches customer service.

Ellen is a team leader in a bank's contact centre. Her team always achieves stand out customer service ratings, so Ellen is often invited to talk at induction programs for new staff where she does a segment on responding to negative customer feedback. Each time she covers the same things: the outcome they are aiming for, what to say, the systems to use, reporting that's required, and escalation processes available when needed.

Directing

Directing involves providing clear authoritative instructions, consistent with a 'command and control' approach. This approach has strong merit in some situations, and yet does not allow for the creation of 'insight': that flash of inspiration that brings together seemingly unconnected concepts to give a new understanding. (Insight is explained further in Chapter 3: How does the *Leader Who Asks* support insight?)

A leader directs when they tell staff what to do in clear and explicit terms, and no negotiation is invited.

Brian is a Commander for the fire brigade. On the fire-ground he assumes the role of 'incident controller'—the lead fire fighter in charge of this emergency incident. It's his job to assess the situation, make fast and informed decisions about how best to address the situation, and then issue clear instructions to all personnel, which he expects to be enacted immediately.

At times, Brian also needs to direct civilians (occupants of commercial or residential buildings, motorists, passers-by, etc.); therefore, the clarity of his messages and his ability to switch presentation styles is critical.

Counselling

Counselling has therapeutic origins and typically involves a focus on the past. While some developmental conversations may reference the past, leaders are not trained counsellors. Where it seems that overly strong emotions are at play, and resolution of the past is required, leaders should refer a person to their organisation's Employee Assistance Program or other professional counselling providers for specialist support.

Belinda noticed that Natalie, normally one of her strongest leaders, had been behaving inconsistently. Belinda was unsure why. Deciding that an informal approach was best, she invited Natalie for a coffee, expressed empathy, reflected her recent observations, and asked Natalie if there was something going on.

Struggling to hold back tears, Natalie told Belinda her husband had been diagnosed with a serious illness, and that he had commenced treatment and wasn't coping well. Natalie was also worried about her three children, and was unsure how to communicate to them the seriousness of their father's situation.

Belinda knew she was out of her depth with this situation, and Natalie was grateful when Belinda told her about the company's Employee Assistance Program, which could provide counselling support. Natalie took up the counselling offer from experienced professionals. Belinda was then able to focus on how best to support Natalie in the workplace. Together they developed a plan that would allow Natalie to take time off when she needed to take her husband to treatment or to support her children.

Coaching

So if all that is *not* coaching, what is?

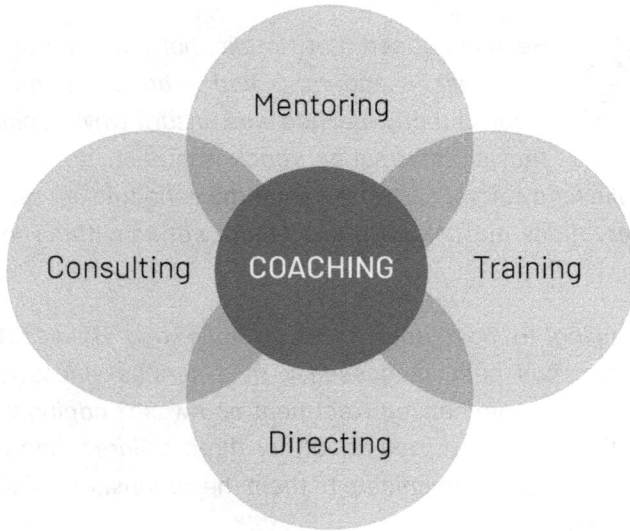

Figure 2: Development strategies of a leader

While coaching draws on some elements of all those styles, in it's own right, it is something different again. Coaching is solution focused—we are seeking an outcome—and is based in the present and future. We may need to visit the past briefly in order to understand the present and create the future.

Sir John Whitmore, considered a pioneer of professional coaching, explains the essence of coaching as: '... unlocking a person's potential to maximise their own performance. It is helping them to learn rather than teaching them'.[6] What's important about this is the assumed potential a coachee has, and that the ownership for learning and development remains with the coachee.

If mentoring is about 'telling' and training is about 'showing', then coaching is about 'asking'. A key distinction of a coaching approach is the use of questions—a coach asks questions that help others develop their own insight and answers. **A coach tells less and asks more.**

The *Leader Who Asks* is not a coach

There are three key areas in which the *leader who asks* is not a traditional coach.

1. **The *leader who asks retains* some influence over the coaching focus.** Coaching in an organisational setting has evolved from both therapeutic and sporting origins. In *Challenging Coaching,* authors John Blakey and Ian Day argue that early organisational coaching took its biggest inspiration from person-centred therapy, which is grounded in the view that the client has vast resources needed for development, and the therapist's role is to guide the client to find their own answers according to the client's own agenda.[7]
   This approach has formed the basis for traditional organisational coaching methods, where the coach has a role of holding the space while the client works things through.

   The *leader who asks* has more influence over of direction of the conversation than a traditional coach might, and coaching by the *leader who asks* is often developmental in nature.

2. **The *leader who asks* may have knowledge.** Another way in which the role of the *leader who asks* may

differ from a professional coach is by having subject matter expertise. While a coach does not need subject matter expertise, coaching leaders will often have knowledge, and may have done the job of the coachee in the recent past. As we will see later, this knowledge often needs to be put aside during a coaching conversation.

3. **The *leader who asks* chooses when to coach (and when not to).** A professional coach coaches—that is their job and that's what they do. The *leader who asks* has a much broader job description, and coaching is not their job. Coaching is simply a tool that a leader will use to achieve KPIs through their team. The *leader who asks* chooses when to coach and when to use other forms of intervention such as those outlined above—and many others—based on the needs of the situation, the people, and the task, in the moment.

The *leader who asks*:

*   draws on coaching qualities to unlock a person's potential to maximise their performance
*   facilitates self-directed learning by asking questions that build awareness and generate insight
*   proactively supports the development of their people by helping people learn rather than teaching them.

How the *Leader Who Asks* leads

Let's not underestimate a coaching approach

It's easy to underestimate the power of a coaching approach and think that coaching skills are for one:one formal conversations only. This would be a mistake.

Coaching skills make formal one:one conversations flow, and the *leader who asks* is much more likely to get an outcome to which both parties are committed. That's only one of the many ways in which coaching skills can be applied. Coaching skills allow a leader to make an instant connection in a quick corridor conversation, and get outcomes that in the past might have taken multiple conversations, over many weeks.

Coaching skills will ensure that the *leader who asks* creates clarity about the intention of a meeting, and is able to facilitate a good conversation where everyone feels heard and has commitment to decisions.

Coaching skills will help the *leader who asks* to coach himself out of overwhelm or through a sticky situation. Selectively using the capacities of coaching will help the *leader who asks* to manage up and be more influential. Coaching skills can be applied in a broad range of leadership challenges.

Culture change needs *Leaders Who Ask* throughout the organisation

Typically, culture change starts at the top, and the ongoing support and modelling of the desired culture by the senior leadership group is critical. It's also critical that leaders throughout the organisation understand the vision, the values,

People are much more
likely to remember
things that they
have worked out for
themselves, than
things their boss
has told them.

and the expected behaviours, and can coach to that throughout the organisation.

Culture is the sum of every little thing we do each day. The *leader who asks* creates culture and change momentum through informal interactions as well as formal conversations.

The *Leader Who Asks* leverages the power of the brain

The *leader who asks* utilises what we know about the brain from studies in neuroscience.

I often hear complaints from leaders along a similar theme: *'I have been over this with her in the past and each time she agrees. Yet each time nothing changes.'* Leaders are frustrated that their good advice is being overlooked and their instructions ignored by members of their team.

So what's going on here? (The clue is in the brain!)

1. **They are hearing you, they just don't care**

    To pay attention (and to change behaviour), the brain needs the right amount of dopamine. Dopamine levels are increased when a person sees relevance in the messages being delivered.[8] If they don't have any ownership over the messages they are receiving, even when they 'hear' you, they just don't care.

2. **There's nothing new, you have said it all before**

    The brain learns best when there is novelty or variety. Are you 'telling' them the same thing in the same way, over and over? I saw a funny cartoon recently. A parent was explaining to a child, in detail, what behaviour was

---

expected on a visit to Grandma's house. The kid was hearing 'blah blah blah'. What are your people hearing?

3. **Their emotional brains are not engaged**

   When you give instructions, they may be listening with their 'rational brain', but this won't necessarily help with recall. Engage their 'emotional brain' to increase the chance they will remember and apply what you have said. Emotions focus attention on the stimulus, and through engaging the amygdala, emotions signal to the brain that an event is significant. This leads to enhanced recall.

Think about your own learning? Under what conditions are you more likely to listen, generate ideas, and take ownership?

So what does this mean? Simply that people are much more likely to remember things—and apply them to other situations—that they have worked out for themselves, than things their boss has told them. The *leader who asks* utilises that understanding.

How does the *Leader Who Asks* support insight?

The fundamental distinction between a coaching approach and many other forms of skill development is the use of asking and not telling.

Many problems can be solved by taking an analytical approach, and systematically working through the problem and possible solutions. The types of problems that are best solved with a coaching approach often require a different way: a new way of thinking about the problem and the solution. The questioning associated with a coaching leadership style helps find a fresh

The simple act
of searching for
our own answers
is rewarding to
the brain.

approach that generates a new understanding, and that's where insight comes in.

When people solve a challenge for themselves—rather than being 'told'—'insight' is involved. Insight is that sudden understanding—a 'Eureka' moment—when the brain takes seemingly unrelated ideas and puts them together in new ways to reach a new understanding.

Insights engage the brain's reward systems and trigger a release of dopamine: a neurotransmitter associated with the brains rewards system known as a 'happy chemical'.[9] The simple act of searching for our own answers is rewarding to the brain.

Insight activates the hippocampus, the area of the brain responsible for long-term memories.[10] Insights are memorable because there is an emotional component; the amygdala—the part of the brain responsible for emotional arousal—is engaged.[11]

Memory is also augmented with insight because we make rich neural connections to things we already know.

Problems solved via insight support application of the solution more broadly. The ability to generalise occurs when we are able to 'recognise new patterns in the problems we encounter and strategies we use to solve them', and to recognise this in subsequent situations.[12] So, one insight can address multiple challenges across different time and context.

Methylation

A little known fact is that I have a science degree, majoring in genetics. (Sadly, I have never made much use of all that knowledge pumped into my head.) There's a concept in genetics referred to as methylation. It's a process where you don't have to change the sequence of the gene to change its function. Instead, a chemical layer or coding turns up or down the activation of a given gene. In other words, by changing the chemical and social conditions, the full expression of the gene ('turning on' the gene, for the non-geneticists among you) can be stimulated.

A while ago, I heard an interesting radio interview with a geneticist whose research was about using the process of methylation to trigger growth in ants. The result was **more** ants of bigger sizes than would otherwise occur, through encouraging the expression of growth genes. Interestingly, the ants' growth does not happen beyond the normal growth range: we don't get 2-foot long ants, but we do get more big ants within the standard range of ant sizes.[13]

What is your leadership methylating? As a leader, which leadership genes are fully expressed under your leadership?

The *leader who asks* 'methylates' **engagement**, **accountability**, and **productivity**, creating the conditions for these attributes to be fully expressed and developed within the 'normal range' of abilities. By adding coaching skills to their leadership toolkit, and bringing more *ask* and less *tell* into their leadership style, the *leader who asks* methylates for a Fearless Culture.

Chapter 4

Building a
Fearless Culture

1

The Fearless Culture

What could be possible when you tell less and ask more? When you give up the need to be in control, and instead utilise the skills and confidence needed to conduct the crucial yet sometimes uncomfortable conversations? What might be enabled when you leverage corridor conversations, lead engaging meetings, and stimulate new ideas in individuals and groups? What could you gain by being able to influence effectively up, down and sideways?

Leadership is tricky. It's challenging and rewarding, and at times, it's fun. (Interestingly, the more skills we have to draw on the more fun leadership becomes!) Building culture is tricky too, and it starts and ends with leadership. Adding coaching skills to your toolkit will help you be brave enough to connect deeply, lead fearlessly, and achieve results that transform—laying down the pathway to a Fearless Culture.

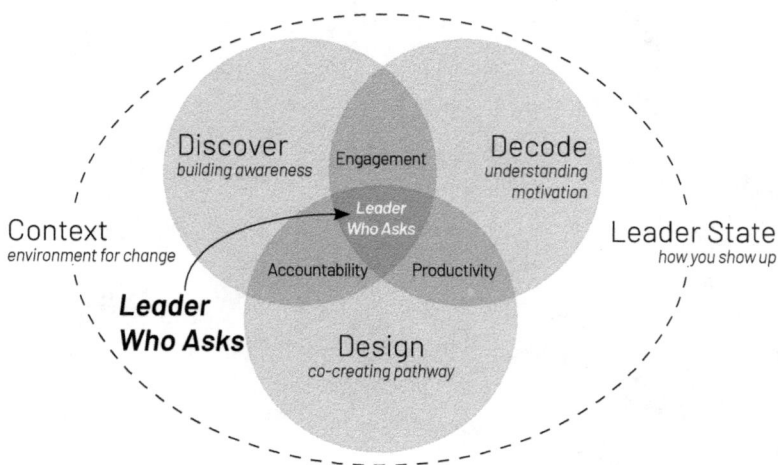

Figure 3: The Fearless Culture (Adapted from model by Armour, Blundell, Cohen, *Developing Direct Reports*, 2015)

Leadership is tricky. It's challenging and rewarding, and at times, it's fun.

So how does asking more and telling less lead to a Fearless Culture? Introducing coaching skills and questioning techniques into a leader's toolkit gives them new ways to engage with, and influence and lead others, as well as extending their capability for self-management.

Let's break it down to the key elements we need to consider.

CONTEXT: Environment for change

Change does not happen in a vacuum. Context shapes everything. The *leader who asks* understands and leverages the environment for change, and is tuned in to their own context as well as the context of the team. Context creates the frame through which the development is shaped and the coaching conversations take place.

DISCOVER: Building awareness

Awareness precedes change. The *leader who asks* knows that discovery is a critical first step—with no awareness, there can be no development. This might be awareness of an individual team member who is being coached, or a whole team. You may be building awareness around a skill gap, a behavioural issue, a flaw in the process, a deliverable running behind schedule, or the outcomes to be achieved from a team meeting.

With awareness comes choice, and the opportunity to make new decisions, form new behaviours, and build a Fearless Culture.

DECODE: Understanding motivation

With awareness, you can progress to supporting the person in understanding their motivation. This requires going beyond the behaviour we see to exploring the intention behind the behaviour.

All behaviour is motivated; it is driven by conscious and below-conscious drivers. The better people (individual and groups) understand their drivers, the more able they are to change.

DESIGN: Co-creating pathway

Awareness and understanding is useful, and yet without action nothing changes. Design is about devising a plan of action. The *leader who asks* supports individuals or teams to create their own pathway, resulting in a plan that is connected to personal and business objectives.

Equally important is supporting the implementation of the plan. The *leader who asks* provides feedback, enhances accountability, and celebrates success.

LEADER STATE: How you show up

How you show up as the *leader who asks* matters more than any coaching framework you might follow (and I say that even though my framework is a good one). Your 'being' is as important as what you know and what you do. Your state matters because who you are in the conversation sets the tone and impacts the outcome. In fact, it's so important there is a whole chapter dedicated to the Leader State.

Let's make it happen

If you would like to develop engagement, accountability, productivity, *and* build a Fearless Culture, let's unpack The Fearless Culture Model so it can guide your conversations and support you in developing your skills as the *leader who asks*.

Chapter 5

The coaching framework

The **leader who asks** brings coaching questions and competencies into their daily leadership.

When we redraw the model in Figure 3, we see it is also a framework for coaching conversations—the 3D model of Coaching. Beginning at the bottom, we discover 'what's the issue?' We then decode 'what's the cause?' And finally, we design a response, confirming 'what's the action?'

The *leader who asks* works with their people to follow this 3-step framework, while maintaining an awareness of how they are showing up themselves (leader state) and the environment for change (the broader context).

Whether you are conducting an end-to-end coaching conversation, a quick corridor catch up, or facilitating a team meeting, the 3D model will provide a framework for your conversation. It will guide your focus at any point, as well as help you understand the type of questions to ask, and when.

The 3D model of coaching

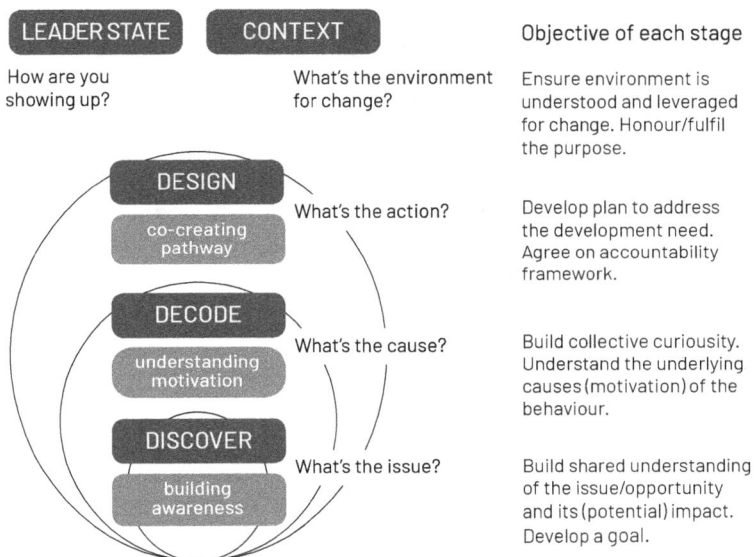

| LEADER STATE | CONTEXT | Objective of each stage |

How are you showing up? | What's the environment for change? | Ensure environment is understood and leveraged for change. Honour/fulfil the purpose.

DESIGN
co-creating pathway
What's the action?
Develop plan to address the development need. Agree on accountability framework.

DECODE
understanding motivation
What's the cause?
Build collective curiousity. Understand the underlying causes (motivation) of the behaviour.

DISCOVER
building awareness
What's the issue?
Build shared understanding of the issue/opportunity and its (potential) impact. Develop a goal.

Figure 4: The 3D Model: A Coaching Framework for The *Leader Who Asks* (Adapted from model by Armour, Blundell, Cohen. *Developing Direct Reports*, 2015)

How you show up—Leader State—is THE most important element of the coaching framework. We have all seen frameworks applied well without success. A coaching structure followed without rapport, and a framework well applied without connection, will not take you towards a Fearless Culture. In this chapter, we will start at CONTEXT, and work through DISCOVER, DECODE and DESIGN. Chapter 7 will focus on LEADER STATE, helping you develop your way of 'being' to maximise the impact of your conversations.

CONTEXT: Environment for change

What's the environment for change?

While the first step in the conversation is DISCOVER, the *leader who asks* is always aware of the importance of context in shaping everything, including environment, behaviour and results. The **leader who asks** remains mindful of what is happening between and around them, and are able to support the people they lead to also develop this understanding.

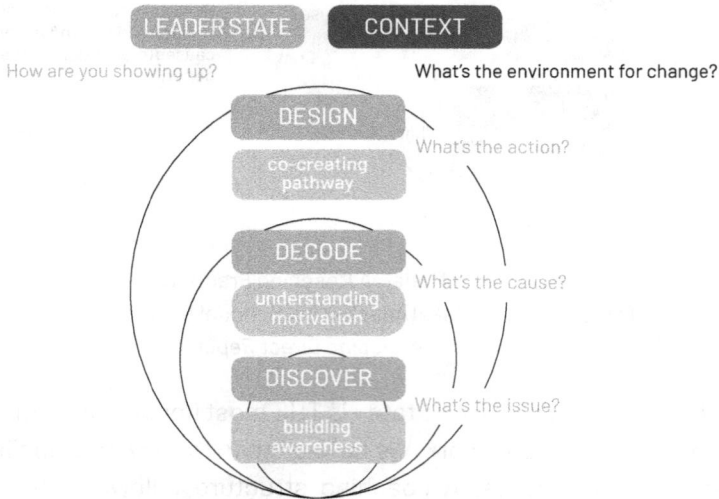

The objective of this stage is to ensure that the environment is understood and leveraged for change, so that you maximise the chance of success.

The context can be anything in the immediate (and sometimes extended) environment that can potentially influence the outcomes for the coachee. Context could include:

- team, organisational and even sector culture

- team dynamics

- leadership style and trust levels

- perceived conflicts of interest

- working relationship between you and the coachee

- coachee's own reputation and/or career goals

- external political, social, technological and environmental landscape

- financial constraints

- organisational priorities

- personal joys or challenges in the coachee's life right now (or even in the past or future)

- your own strengths and weaknesses, beliefs and values.

Finding out more about the context will help refine the objective of the conversation, and may influence how you might approach the conversation. Consider the following situations. What might your approach be if you just considered the initial context and then, if you obtained 'more context'? How might that shift if you, instead, uncovered the 'alternative context'?

Initial Context	More Context	Alternative Context
Gail's performance has dropped over the past three months.	Gail's performance has dropped over the past three months. Her husband has just ended their nine-year marriage, leaving her with the two children.	Gail's performance has dropped over the past three months. There seems to be tension between her and two of her colleagues.
John is new to his role. He joined the company last week.	John is new to his role. He joined the company last week. He knows the sector well because his last role was similar to this, but for a competitor. He knew most of the people in the team before he arrived.	John is new to his role. He joined the company last week. This is his first 'real job' having graduated three months ago from university.
Your team has just missed a minor project milestone.	Your team has just missed a minor project milestone. It's the first one it has missed for 12 months, and everything else is running on track.	Your team has just missed a minor project milestone. This is the fourth milestone missed in the past three months and project delivery could be at risk.
The Customer Service Team Leader asks you what he should do about the *Johnson* account.	The Customer Service Team Leader asks you what he should do about the *Johnson* account. This account is strategically important to the company, and the CEO is taking a keen interest in how it progresses.	The Customer Service Team Leader asks you what he should do about the *Johnson* account. This is a small account, and it's the fourth time this team leader has asked you a similar question so far this week.

Initial Context	More Context	Alternative Context
Leon has received an MBA scholarship opportunity, and he would like your advice on whether to accept it.	Leon has received an MBA scholarship opportunity, and he would like your advice on whether to accept it. He is a stand-out performer and future CEO material. He has embraced formal learning opportunities offered to him in the past.	Leon has received an MBA scholarship opportunity, and he would like your advice on whether to accept it. He has recently declined to be interviewed for two significant promotions, saying that for the next three years he wants a better balance between family and career.
Your peer has been unsupportive in exec meetings.	Your peer has been unsupportive in exec meetings. A significant legislative change is resulting in significant change across her part of the business.	Your peer has been unsupportive in exec meetings. You suspect the CEO is having performance conversations with her.
You have received a complaint about Malcom's brash communication style, and you would like his manager to address this.	You have received a complaint about Malcom's brash communication style, and you would like his manager to address this. The manager made an allegation of bullying against Malcom in the past.	You have received a complaint about Malcom's brash communication style, and you would like his manager to address this. The culture of that whole team is brash.

What shifts did you notice as the context changed? How might you approach each version of the conversation?

'Sometimes your greatest strength can emerge as a weakness if the context changes,' observed Indian cricket commentator and TV presenter Harsha Bhogle. That is definitely the case when we consider the people we work with, and our role as the *leader who asks*.

Aaron was a highly successful project developer in the IT&T space. Brought in on contract by CIOs when it looked like the project wasn't possible, Aaron always made it happen. He was in demand—driven, result-focused, highly successful and very well paid ... until he moved contexts.

Ready for a change of pace, Aaron took a role setting up and leading a projects group in a large community health provider. His task-over-people approach and win-at-all-costs mentality didn't work the relationship-based context of a community organisation. After only three months, people were leaving his team, key stakeholders were having difficulty engaging him, and projects were falling behind.

Aaron had not recognised that he had shifted contexts, and his leadership style needed to shift too. The executive who recruited him had not recognised this either, and so did not coach Aaron on adapting to the new context.

In order to understand the application of the 3D model, let's follow Debra as she coaches Rory. Debra is the CEO of a hospital, and she has some concerns about how the CFO (Rory) is interacting with his colleagues, and in particular how his use of humour is preventing the executive team from progressing important conversations.

Debra was keeping the broader context in mind when she was contemplating the conversation she wanted to have with Rory. She considered the current culture of the executive team and the dynamics between individual team members. She thought through timing: it was currently a period of relative quiet for the organisation and so both she and Rory would have the headspace for this conversation. She was conscious of the board's desire for her to strengthen the executive team to enable her to take a more strategic focus. Rory's own career goals and potential were top of mind for her, as was the compatibility between Debra and Rory's leadership styles. All these factors influenced the way in which Debra approached Rory.

CONTEXT: Strategies to understand the environment for change

Ways in which you might build your awareness of the context include:

- noticing the key influences, dynamics and relationships at play in the coachee's professional world

- considering what is happening in the wider organisation and/or the industry that could be impacting on this situation

- looking for patterns (eg trends in behaviour or results)

- examining your relationship with the coachee(s) and how this might impact on the dynamics within the conversation

- reflecting on what else might be impacting the coachees' personal context (eg pressures outside the workplace)

- questioning to bring anything of significance to the coachee's attention.

CONTEXT: Outcomes

The outcomes the *leader who asks* is seeking from this stage are:

1. clarity on the most significant dynamics and influences on the coachee and his environment

2. understanding of relevant considerations or constraints in the environment, including what might be going on for them personally

3. awareness of the need to tailor responses to the context.

DISCOVER: Building awareness

What's the issue?

Awareness precedes change. The *leader who asks* knows that discovery is a critical first step—with no awareness, there can be no development. This might be awareness of one person or of a group. You may be building awareness around a skill gap, a behavioural issue, a process flaw, a deliverable running behind schedule, or the outcomes to be achieved from a team meeting.

Whether the conversation is a full coaching conversation about behavioural change, or whether it's a short corridor conversation about a process issue, awareness of the situation and a definition of the problem are needed first.

With awareness
comes choice, and the
opportunity to make
new decisions, form
new behaviours, and
build a Fearless Culture.

With awareness comes choice, and the opportunity to make new decisions, form new behaviours, and build a Fearless Culture. Helping build awareness is a critical role of the *leader who asks*.

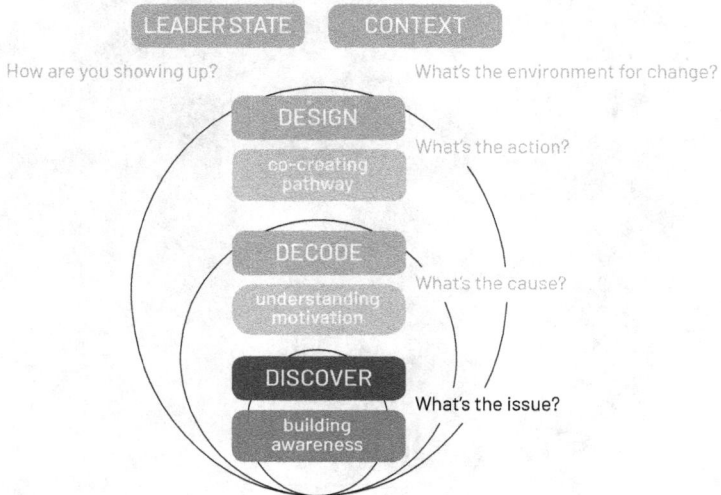

Charles F Kettering was an American inventor, businessman, engineer, and head of research at General Motors from 1920 to 1947. He famously claimed that 'A problem well stated is a problem half solved' and that is certainly the case in a coaching conversation.

The challenge in DISCOVERY is that the *leader who asks* and the coachee often don't know exactly what the problem is. And sometimes when we think we know what the problem is, we are wrong. The more awareness we can build around the challenge being faced, the closer we are to defining the problem.

Behavioural change in others is one of the most challenging areas for the *leader who asks*. When we consider coaching a staff member on a behavioural issue, they may lack awareness about the extent to which the problem actually exists.

 **Back to Rory (CFO) and Debra (CEO) ...** *Rory is quick-witted and always ready with a joke. He knows that one of his strengths is his ability to diffuse a tense situation with humour. Rory lacks awareness of the downside of his tendency to tell a joke—that the growth of the executive team he is part of is stunted because he breaks any tension with a joke before breakthroughs can be reached in challenging conversations.*

Rory did not know that there was a problem that needed attention. The first challenge for Debra was to build Rory's awareness of the impact of his behaviour. She coached him to see that his tendency to short-circuit tense situations meant that conversations necessary to executive team development were being avoided, and this meant that underlying issues were being swept under the carpet and not resolved.

Through examples that Debra was able to share with him (after first seeking his permission to do so), Rory was able to see the impact his behaviour was having on the executive team, on his own reputation and potentially on his career. (Rory aspires to take on a CEO role.)

Rory and Debra agreed that his goal was to allow challenging conversations in the team to develop and progress, and avoid the temptation to crack jokes to restore his own levels of comfort.

The objectives of DISCOVER are to build a shared understanding of the issue (or opportunity) and its (potential) impact, and to develop a goal for the conversation. The *leader who asks* works with the coachee to build awareness of the issue and/or of the need for change.

DISCOVER: Strategies to understand the issue

Ways in which you might build awareness include:

- exploring the full scope of the issue (or opportunity) at hand
- checking if the coachee is getting the results they want with this current behaviour or strategy
- teasing out the impact of this issue on:
    - » other people: peers, clients, senior staff, their reports, external stakeholders, etc.
    - » business results: team, division, company
    - » themselves: reputation, leadership brand, future opportunities
    - » how others perceive the coachee and/or the issue
    - » the possible consequences of taking and not taking action.
- establishing the intended outcome of the conversation or the goal to be achieved
- questioning to expand their perspective
- encouraging the coachee to seek feedback from others (colleagues, direct reports, stakeholders)
- reflecting back your observations

- encouraging self-reflection.

DISCOVER: Outcomes

The outcomes the *leader who asks* is seeking from this stage are:

1. clarity on the issue (or opportunity) at hand, and the potential impact

2. buy-in for coaching conversations and being open to explore new ways of achieving their outcome

3. agreement on the goal.

DECODE: Understanding motivation

What's the cause?

With awareness and the problem clearly defined, we are ready to move onto understanding motivation and exploring the cause of the issue.

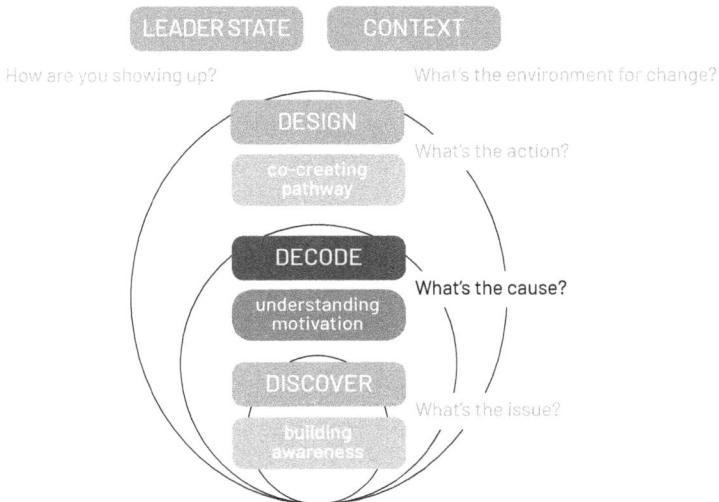

In my 30s, I took up running for the first time. It was very slow going, initially running 100 m then walking 100 m etc. until I was finally able to run 5 km. Yeah for me! After a couple of months, I developed knee pain that slowed and then stopped my running, even making walking hard. A sports physio treated my knee with very little response, so further tests were prescribed.

It turned out that I had a problem with dysfunctional nerves in my right foot, and no amount of knee treatment was going to fix that. Understanding the underlying driver of the problem was crucial to addressing it and getting me back running again.

Back to Rory (CFO) and Debra (CEO) ... *Having agreed that Rory's goal was to allow tense conversations to develop and progress, and avoid the temptation to crack jokes to restore his levels of comfort, Debra asked Rory questions that helped him build insight into why he felt the need to make jokes.*

Rory was uncomfortable with conflict, and whenever he sensed conflict was possible, he immediately moved to humour as a line of defence. Having this new insight about himself, and talking through with Debra the worst case scenarios of what conflict could arise within the executive team, Rory was ready (if somewhat tentative) to move forward.

Sometimes a problem is not what it seems and understanding the actual cause is critical to determining the solution. The role of the *leader who asks* is to help the coachee understand what is really going on.

DECODE: Strategies to understand the cause

Ways in which you might support the coachee to understand their motivation include:

- getting behind the immediately obvious by asking questions
- offering your observations (carefully!)
- allowing the space for thought and encouraging self-reflection
- creating the conditions for insight (see Chapter 3)
- validating their inside intention as positive and perhaps not yet productive
- helping the coachee understand that there are other ways to achieve their outcomes
- giving them confidence that they can build the new skills required.

DECODE: Outcomes

The outcomes the *leader who asks* is seeking from this stage are:

1. collective curiosity
2. understanding the underlying causes (motivation) of the problem or situation.

DESIGN: Co-creating pathway

What's the action?

Nothing changes without action. Designing a pathway forward creates the roadmap and the measures for change.

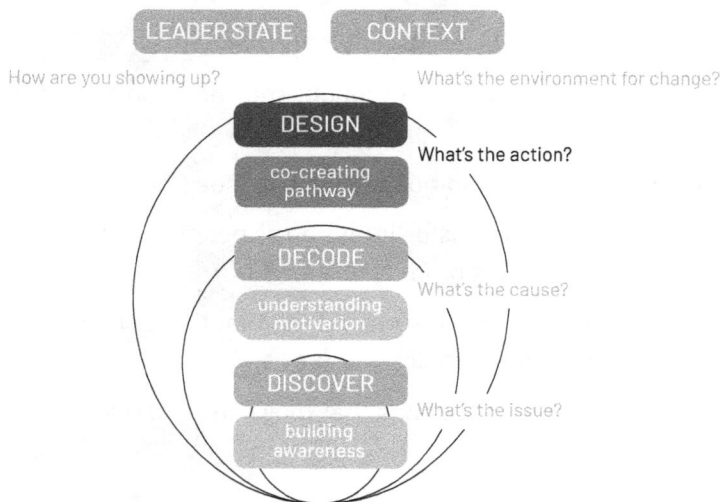

Back to Rory (CFO) and Debra (CEO) ... *Rory and Debra both knew that if Rory was going to change a behavioural strategy he had been using unconsciously for most of his life, he needed a plan and support to follow the plan. Guided by Debra's encouragement and questions, Rory developed an approach for showing up differently in the executive meetings, including becoming more in tune with how he was feeling. He worked out tactics he would use instead of cracking jokes when he felt uncomfortable. They agreed on the best ways for Debra to support the new behaviours, as well as how and when they would check in on progress.*

> *Debra was very conscious of allowing Rory to lead this part*
> *of the conversation, even when she thought Rory had chosen*
> *one less powerful strategy. She could see that if Rory fully*
> *committed to his 7/10 plan, he would get a better outcome than*
> *a mediocre commitment to a 9/10 plan she might insist on.*

I am sure you can think of a personal situation where you identified a challenge and understood what was driving it, but took no action. Not surprisingly, no change resulted. Let's ensure our coachees move beyond understanding the drivers to implementing action by supporting them to develop a plan to address the identified problem.

Notice that DESIGN is about **co-creating** a pathway. The collaborative nature and intent of designing a development plan is critical and should be led by the coachee. Development actions 'assigned' by you are unlikely to succeed, as there will be little ownership. When the plan comes from them, it results in increased accountability. Your role primarily is guidance and support rather than authoring the plan.

DESIGN: Strategies to determine the action

Ways in which you might co-create a pathway include:

- asking open questions to get them generating possible actions

- exploring what actions <u>could</u> be taken. 'Could' opens possibilities and keeps the conversation lighter. 'Could' is for ideation. (See Chapter 6: The Coaching Question Menu)

- determining what action <u>will</u> be taken. 'Will' narrows options and leads to the commitment we need at the end of a coaching conversation. This is where you can use closed questions. (See Chapter 6: The Coaching Question Menu)

- discussing the level and type of support they need from you to enact their development plan

- providing introductions to new people from whom they can learn, and other resources and references like books, journals, videos

- agreeing on an accountability framework so you are both clear on your roles and how/when to follow up on progress.

DESIGN: Outcomes

The outcomes the *leader who asks* is seeking from this stage are:

1. a clear action plan that the coachee is committed to achieving (with accountability measures)

2. articulated and agreed support role for the *leader who asks*

3. shared belief in their ability to progress.

LEADER STATE

How are you showing up?

Many coaching books and programs teach a coaching model: what to say, when to say it, and what to do next—as if that were the critical factor. While a framework is important and gives structure to the conversation, it's NOT the most important thing.

Your STATE is the critical factor here. In fact, it's so important that when I work with leaders in the *Leader Who Asks* Program, we focus on the Leader State and the competencies that underpin the Leader State, almost as much as developing their skills using a coaching framework.

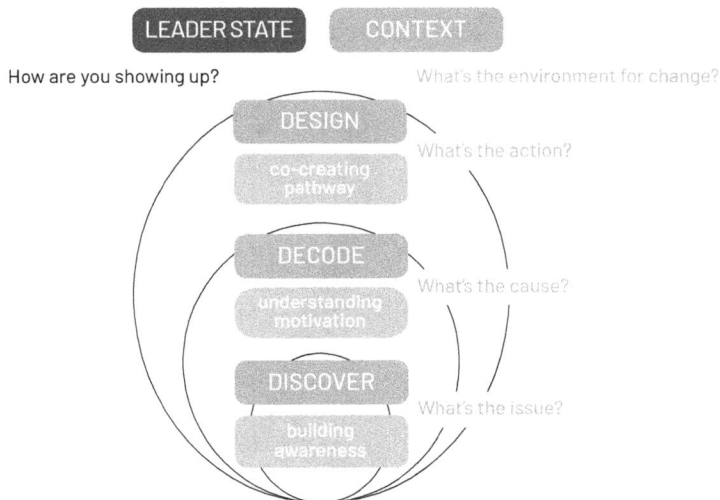

Chapter 7 of this book is dedicated to helping you develop your state as the **leader who asks**.

Coaching framework summary

The *leader who asks* is mindful about asking and telling, and making a conscious decision in the moment about what will best serve the person, the situation and the task.

The 3D model can be used in one:one conversations or with groups, formally or informally. You might use the 3D model end-to-end, or you might just dip in and out when you need to, remembering that your state will always trump the 'structure' of the conversation.

Chapter 6

The coaching question menu

If you are to move from the leader who tells, to the *leaders who ask*, having some good questions at your fingertips will help.

Use these questions as an aid to assess the conversation. I have included a range of questions you could ask at each stage of the 3D model. Many of them are different ways of asking the same thing, and some questions will suit your communication style more than others. You may want to copy these pages and keep them with you as you build your 'asking' muscle.

As you practice, you will develop your own asking style. Very soon, you will be able to formulate your own questions in the moment, utilising the coachee's language and building on the conversation.

CONTEXT: Questions to develop understanding

What is the environment?

Objectives: 1) Clarify the most significant dynamics and influences on the coachee and his environment. 2) Understand considerations or constraints in the environment. 3) Build awareness of the need to tailor responses to the context.

Note: These are reflective questions for you to consider. You may decide to bring some of these into the coaching conversation.

How might the culture of the team impact this plan?

How might your organisational culture impact this plan?

What external environmental factors need to be taken into account with this plan?

How does this conversation relate to the coachee's KPIs?

Who are the key stakeholders? What impact might they have on the outcome?

What are the forces for change in the current environment?

What are the forces opposing change in the current environment?

How can the current environment be leveraged to support development?

What patterns do you see in the coachee's behaviour/results?

What might be going on in the coachee's personal world that could impact this conversation and/or plan?

DISCOVER: Questions to build awareness

What's the issue?

<u>Objectives</u>: 1) Build shared understanding of the issue (or opportunity) and the potential impact. 2) Develop buy-in for coaching. 3) Agree on the goal.

<u>Questions for opening</u>

So what's on your mind?

What is an/the issue you would like to work on?

What's the best use of our time today?

What would you like to be different by the time we have finished our conversation/meeting?

What are we here to achieve today?

What would you like to gain from this meeting?

What would you like to have by the end of this conversation?

What do you REALLY want?

What do you want to happen as a result of this conversation?

What makes this goal important?

What is important about this goal that you need to share with me?

What would other people like to achieve?

In the long term, what is your goal in relation to this issue? What is the timeframe?

From where you are now, what would be a first step that you could feel good about?

Questions for focusing

What is happening that you don't want to happen?

What would you like to happen instead? What would be the result of that?

If you could summarise the problem in two sentences, what would you say?

If you had to put the challenge in a 140-character tweet, what would it be?

What's not working here?

Questions for broadening awareness

What do other people (stakeholders, clients, colleagues) think is happening here?

What is the impact of this on other people? (eg peers, clients, senior staff, their reports, external stakeholders)

What else bothers you? ... And what else? ... And what else?

What could you do to reward yourself/them?

What will be the evidence that you have achieved this?

What is the impact of this on business results? (eg team, division, company)

What is the impact of this on you personally/professionally?

How do others perceive you/the situation?

Is this approach/behaviour currently getting the results you want?

What behaviours are derailing your performance, and what are the consequences?

How do you know that?

How are you doing in relation to <challenge>?

Thinking about <habit/behaviour>, how well is that serving you right now?

What is the impact of this on your reputation/leadership brand/future opportunities?

Where did you get your information? How do you know that is correct?

What do you think they are thinking?

What's the worst-case scenario here?

What is the concern that lies behind the dissatisfaction?

What's your ideal time frame on this?

By when would you want that to be the case?

What would you want people to say at your funeral about the impact you have had?

DECODE: Questions to understand motivation

What's the cause?

Objectives: 1) Build collective curiosity. 2) Understand the underlying causes (motivations) of the problem or the situation.

What is the reality of the current situation as you see it?

What action/steps have you taken so far?

How often does this happen?

What do you see/hear/feel happening?

What other factors are relevant?

What need is behind your/their behaviour?

What do you think is driving their behaviour?

What is the result of all that?

How would your colleague/boss/partner explain this situation?

What help do you need for the work to get done?

What do you think your superpower is?

What might be the flipside of your key strengths?

What activities have meaning for you?

How can that skill help you in the workplace?

How have you/we contributed to that?

What could you/we have done differently to avoid the situation?

What could we have done to plan for this better?

How much of this situation do you feel is within your control?

Can you help me to understand what's behind that for you?

What, if any, internal obstacle(s) or personal resistance(s) do you have to taking action?

If you had to state a purpose for your life, what would it be?

If you had to state a purpose for this project, what would it be?

Thinking about <behaviour>, what was your highest positive intention?

Thinking about <situation>, what were you trying to achieve? What happened instead? What did you learn from that?

How would you need to think/feel/believe/decide differently to get a different result?

What are you afraid of?

What is the excuse you have used to yourself so far for not achieving this?

Imagine it were six months from now, what would you describe if you looked back to today?

DESIGN: Questions to co-create a pathway

What's the action?

Objectives: 1) Develop an action plan with accountability measures. 2) Identify and agree how the *leader who asks* can support change. 3) Build a shared belief in their ability to progress.

Note the use of 'could' rather than 'will'. 'Could' opens possibilities and keeps the conversation lighter. 'Will' narrows options as it infers a commitment, and that comes at the end of this stage of the conversation.

Questions to develop options to move forward

What could be done to achieve the outcome you are seeking?*

What are some of the ways you could approach this?*

What could you do as a first step?*

What else could you do? ... And what else*

What's one more thing you could do?*

If you were guaranteed to succeed, what would you do?

What could you do if you could start again today, what would you do?*

What would you tell me to do if I were in your situation?

What advice would you give to someone in this exact same situation?

What possibilities for action do you see?

If there were another option, what would it be?

What have you seen work in situations like this in the past?

Who do you know who does this stuff well? What might they advise you if they were here?

Questions to gain commitment to action

What will be done to achieve the goal?

What option(s) do you think will work best?

What action has the most clarity and energy for you?

Which option(s) do you choose?

What specifically are you willing to commit to? When will you start/finish?

What might get in the way of this? What will you do to prevent/overcome this?

Who might be able to help?

What support do you need and from whom?

What can I (as coach) do to support you?

How can I help you work on this?

What commitment (scale of 1–10) do you have to completing these agreed actions? What could you do to raise this to an 8 (9 or 10)?

What are the next steps you are committing to take?

Questions for accountability

What do you need from me? From others?

How will you measure success?

What if you did
know the answer?
What would it be?

How will we track achievement?

When will we check in again? How often?

How often do you want feedback from me? In what way?

Wildcards and useful non-questions

<u>Wild card questions that can be used at any time</u>

Imagine you were an <engineer/actor/politician/football player/CEO>, how would you consider this situation and the possibilities?

For when they say they don't' know: What if you did know the answer? What would it be?

For when they want you to tell them what to do: What do you think I am going to advise you to do?

For when they want you to tell them what to do: What is the question you don't want me to ask you right now?

For when you are unsure where to go next: What is the next question I need to ask you right now?

<u>'Non-questions' to deepen their thinking and understanding</u>

Tell me more about that.

I am curious about <behaviour/action/comment just made>.

Help me to understand <behaviour/action/comment just made>.

Tell me more about your thinking on <behaviour/action/comment just made>.

Talk me through how you came to decide <decision made>.

LEADER STATE: Questions to build your self-perception

How are you showing up?

Objective: Understand the potential impact your state could have on the conversation.

Note: These are reflective questions for you and not for the coachee.

How are you 'showing up' in this coaching conversation?

What do you believe to be true about this person? How might this be impacting your ability to coach them?

What do you believe to be true about this situation? What impact could this have on how you act in the conversation?

What do you need to let go of right now, to be fully present in this coaching conversation?

On a scale of 1–5, how curious are you about this person and their potential? What could you do to scale that curiosity up?

How well are you prepared to listen during this conversation?

What would help you focus more on intention and less on behaviour right now?

How ready are you to sit with uncertainty and ambiguity?

What biases might you have that could be preventing you seeing this person as they really are or as they could be?

What has happened between you and this person/group in the recent past that might impact this conversation?

What power/political dynamics may be at play that could impact this conversation?

Chapter 7

LEADER STATE: How you show up matters

How are you showing up?

Your state, as the *leader who asks* will influence the success of any coaching conversation (or any conversation at all!). You are part of the problem as well as a key to the solution. Before you follow a coaching process, you need to be comfortable with who you 'are' as a coaching leader. The question to ask yourselves is 'how am I showing up?'

Once you have built our awareness about our state, we can move into a coaching conversation.

There are 12 core competencies for the *leader who asks*, and these can be grouped into the three areas of:

- **Doing:** The basic approaches you are taking.
- **Knowing**: The understandings you have.
- **Being:** The personal paradigms you operate within.

As we think about these three areas, we can divide our competencies into capabilities that are more focused on:

- **You:** Yourself as the *leader who asks*.
- **Them:** The person or people you are coaching.
- **Space:** The environment—metaphoric 'space'—in which you coach.
- **Relationship:** The relationships you build with those you coach.

The seven competencies marked with a box are the most important: Listening, Courage, Focus, Curiosity, Questions, Empathy and Purpose. These core competencies are critical to being an effective *leader who asks*; in fact, they are important

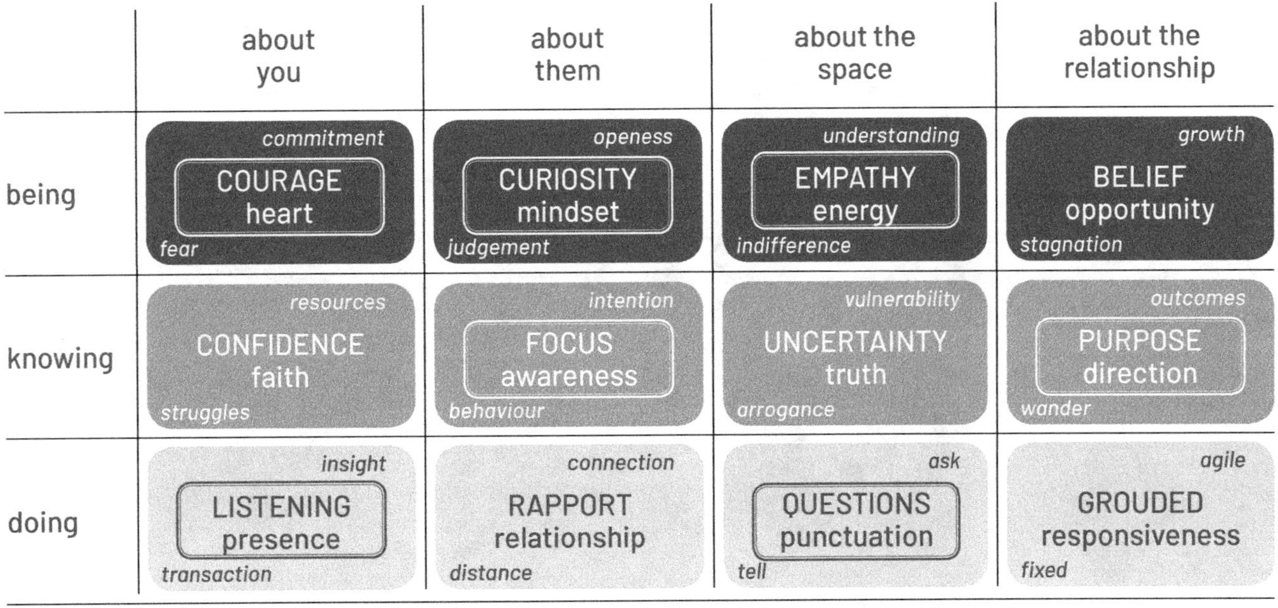

	about you	about them	about the space	about the relationship
being	*commitment* COURAGE heart *fear*	*openess* CURIOSITY mindset *judgement*	*understanding* EMPATHY energy *indifference*	*growth* BELIEF opportunity *stagnation*
knowing	*resources* CONFIDENCE faith *struggles*	*intention* FOCUS awareness *behaviour*	*vulnerability* UNCERTAINTY truth *arrogance*	*outcomes* PURPOSE direction *wander*
doing	*insight* LISTENING presence *transaction*	*connection* RAPPORT relationship *distance*	*ask* QUESTIONS punctuation *tell*	*agile* GROUNDED responsiveness *fixed*

Figure 5: Core competencies of the *Leader Who Asks*

You are part of the
problem as well as a
key to the solution.

for any leader. Chapters 8–11 explain each in turn, and provides 'Questions for the coaching leader' to provoke your thinking about how you might develop each competency.

Caution: As a leader you are heard differently

A few weeks after Graham took up a new CEO role, he casually thought aloud to a few people in the office about the physical layout of the office reception area, curious about why it was laid out that way. Later that afternoon, he left on an interstate trip.

When Graham returned a few days later, he was surprised to find the office layout had completely changed. When he enquired as to why, he was bemused to hear: 'We did what you asked.'

As the CEO, Graham was being 'heard' differently, and it wasn't until his debrief with me that he realised that. Now, Graham is more explicit in his communication, making it overtly clear when he is thinking aloud, asking questions of enquiry, or issuing an instruction.

Sue Desmond-Hellmann, CEO of the Bill & Melinda Gates Foundation, talked about avoiding 'CEO disease'.[14,15] She was asked: 'How do you remain accessible to people and not allow that sense of "she's different from me" to seep in?' She concluded:

- by having family or friends who help you make sure you don't take yourself too seriously

- by inviting the hard questions, and feedback (positive and negative), and thanking people for their willingness to be critical

- by being overt on how you operate: 'I made sure people in the company knew that I asked questions because I was interested, not because I thought there was something wrong'

- by being aware, that as CEO, you are treated differently.

As a leader, you are heard differently. Your state matters. Managing your state will help you avoid 'CEO disease' and build productive coaching relationships.

As a leader, you are
heard differently.

Chapter 8

LEADER STATE:
About you

Listening

Googling 'listening skills for leaders' returns 3,160,000 results. This is clearly a topic of interest. A US Department of Labor study found that government managers spend up to 55% of their time listening, a figure consistent with other research studies done.[16]

So obviously with so much written about listening, and leaders spending half their time doing it, we must be pretty good at it, right? Well no ... not really!

When I train leaders in coaching skills, listening is often the competency they struggle with most. When I demonstrate a coaching conversation from the front of the training room, there are always one or two people who will call out solutions for the person I am coaching, even though they aren't directly in the conversation. These leaders find it impossible to sit and listen without providing the answer.

To provide immediate answers—to be of service—is a strong drive. Many leaders have been promoted into leadership roles initially because of their subject matter expertise or strong technical skills. They are used to providing answers, and in the past have been recognised and rewarded for this, both formally and informally. Jumping in proactively with solutions might be part of their leadership persona. When promoted to more senior leadership roles, holding off on providing ideas and useful advice and truly listen can be a challenge.

Think back to conversations you have had recently with your line manager, or anyone else who could act as a coach in relation to you. Were there times when you were provided with answers for which you weren't ready? And other times when you felt truly heard? What was the difference?

So obviously with so much written about listening, we must be pretty good at it, right?

I was working one:one with a client recently. It was a new coaching relationship and she had a lot of pent up energy and tension. She talked and talked .... And then she stopped, thought for a moment, smiled and said, 'Shit, it's good to be honest and listened to without judgement'. After that, she was calmer and we were able to address her needs.

Listening—truly listening—gives you presence in the conversation to which other people notice and respond. Being fully present and showing up completely, makes this conversation more than a transaction and unleashes potential for insight.

The 3 golden rules of listening for the *Leader Who Asks*

1. 80–20 talk time.
2. Use their language.
3. Allow the silence.

1) 80–20 talk time. When I turn on my Bluetooth phone head set, a digital lady tells me in a clear voice 'You have 5 hours of talk time available'. What if, when I put on my coaching mindset, that same voice told me 'You have 20% of talk time available'? What would that do for the balance between my talking and listening?

Leaders—almost all of us—tend to talk too much and listen too little. If you are doing more than 20% of the talking, you are probably not coaching. The more listening you do, the more awareness you will facilitate in others, and the more trust you will build.

2) Use their language. In listening skills 101 (active listening), we are taught to paraphrase what others tell us, then play it back to ensure (and demonstrate) that we have understood. While this might be useful in some contexts, it's less useful for the *leader* *who asks*, as our coachee's words have special meaning to them. Words are at best an approximation of what a person means to communicate. When we paraphrase, we can take the person further away from their original meaning. Using different words can disrupt their flow of thinking.

Instead, in coaching we practice attentive listening—listening for the coachee's words and using those words. If the goal is unlocking their potential to maximise their own performance, then using their language will keep them in flow.

3) Allow the silence. The coaching leader listens while others are speaking. *And* they listen while others are quiet. When you ask somebody a question and they're silent, it's usually a good sign that they're thinking. It's not an uncomfortable silence, so avoid the temptation to fill the space.

Helping too hard at the trade show

In the trade show area of an industry conference I was speaking at, one of the exhibitors was running a competition. The objective was to put 100 g of salt into a cup. The closest person to 100 g was the winner. The exhibitor challenged me to have a go. Why not? Being the only 'competitor' in the immediate vicinity at the time, I began to 'think out loud' my process of working out how much salt I needed to spoon into the cup. The exhibitor hosting the table immediately offered to give me a clue. I had to say 'no' twice to stop her.

Turns out that my process was pretty good. When the scales revealed I had put 97g of salt in the cup, I won a prize. I never win prizes, so I was pretty chuffed. Would I have felt so pleased with myself if I won after being given a clue? Of course not!

How often do we do this as leaders? 'Help' too hard? Give people clues that rob them of the reward that comes from working it out for themselves? (And how often do we do this as parents?) Let them think and allow the silence.

Be aware of different listening preferences

Being aware of listening preferences will maximise the impact of your communication.

Neutral communicators focus on the specific words that are spoken. They are likely to speak in a monotone fashion and be relatively inexpressive in their facial gestures. As an observer, it can be difficult to determine what they are thinking without asking them.

Affective communicators are tuned into emotions and non verbal signals including body language, facial gestures, voice speed and tone in conversations. The choice of words is less important for them.

Miscommunication is possible between these two communication preferences. If you are a neutral communicator, you will be focused more on the word choice of a more effectively communicating coachee, than on their gestures and tone. This may cause you to miss non-verbal cues and not receive the whole communication message.

If you are an affective communicator, the liveliness of your communication may be distracting for a more neutral communicator, and you might be left guessing what they are thinking as you will not be able to 'read' that on their face.

Listening is such an important skill that books have been written on that topic alone. An excellent book for the *leader who asks* is my good friend Oscar Trimboli's, *Deep Listening: Impact beyond words*.[17] Oscar also has an excellent podcast on Deep Listening that you can find on iTunes.

Listening: Questions for the *leader who asks*

1. *How well would your people say you listen? What suggestions for improvement would they offer?*

2. *Thinking about your last Performance Management conversation with your manger: What amounts did they speak, and listen? How heard did you feel?*

3. *Thinking about your last developmental conversation with someone in your team: What amounts did they and you speak? How well did you listen? How heard do you think they felt?*

4. *How is your 'talk time'? Is it close to 80:20? In coaching conversations, how much are you listening, and how much are you speaking?*

5. *What do you need to let go of to achieve 80:20 talk time?*

6. *What gets in the way of your listening?*

7. *Who do you know who listens well? What could you gain by developing your skill to that level?*

8. *Who do you know who achieves 80:20 talk time? What can you learn from them?*

9. *What prevents you from allowing the silence? What would you need to believe to be more comfortable with silence?*

10. *What meaning do you give 'silence' in a conversation? How might that meaning be getting in the way of your listening?*

11. *If you didn't need to provide answers, how could that free up your conversations?*

12. *How can you calm your inner dialogue so that you are ready and able to listen more effectively?*

13. *Do you sometimes find it hard to resist the temptation to 'help too hard'? If yes, what is driving your need to help? What do you need to shift in order to be more mindful and strategic with your helping? How could you do that?*

14. *If you listened, what might you 'hear' that you otherwise might miss?*

15. *What is your communication preference – effective or neutral? How can you build your communication flexibility around this?*

Confidence

Imagine in any discussion you encounter, having the faith that you will have access to the conversational resources you need. What would that give you?

As the *leader who asks*, you can offer support that generates powerful insights even when you are unsure what specifically is going on for the coachee. When much is unknown and the answers aren't obvious, it is confidence that gives the *leader who asks* faith to continue.

Confidence allows you to relax into the conversation and show up completely—bringing your full heart. Confidence unlocks access to hidden personal resources; it's almost like a magic dust that makes anything possible. And given the phenomenon that is emotional contagion (more on that later), when you are confident, the people you are with will feel more comfortable too.

Imagine these scenarios, enabled by confidence:

1. When a few players are dominating a team meeting, and others are not being heard, you are able to bring out valuable contributions from everyone.

2. In a negotiation, when there seems to be underlying competing interests, you know how to align the parties and bring the negotiation back on track.

3. You are able to elicit feedback from people after an 'all-staff update', where in the past there may have been a deafening silence in the question time offered after the briefing.

4. You are okay to sit in the discomfort of a challenging performance conversation, knowing you have the strategies to move the conversation forward at the right time.

Without a level of confidence, coaching conversations can feel like a struggle.

But what is confidence? Writing in a Harvard Business Review blog, leadership author, researcher and academic Rosabeth Moss Kanter defines confidence as 'the sweet spot between despair and arrogance'.[18] *The Confidence Code* by authors Katty Kay and Claire Shipman offers a definition of confidence as 'being prepared to fail'.[19] Both of these definitions serve our purpose as the *leader who asks*.

Practice some more.

Confidence in your skill set, or in a way of being in a particular type of situation, is something that grows over time and with repeated application. It's not something you typically start out with, so if you experience a lack of confidence, keep going. The more you coach, the more you will build your confidence.

Confidence can be taken from one context to another. In my mid-20s, endurance cycling (Audax) was my exercise (and entertainment too, if you can believe that) of choice. The first time I rode 600 km within the 40-hour maximum time to complete, I realised that endurance sport is much more about fitness and focus of the mind, than athleticism of the body. For the next year, anytime I was up against an insurmountable challenge (personal, work, exercise—anything), I remembered that if I could cycle 600 kms in 36 hours, I could do anything.

Five tips for building confidence in your coaching approach:

1. **Practice:** As you use your coaching skills more and more, your confidence will increase.

2. **Be prepared to 'fail':** Try things out. Keep going and learn along the way.

3. **Start small and safe:** Try out one or two coaching questions. Build your confidence using them and then extend your reach.

4. **Transfer confidence** from another context.

5. **Practice some more:** Did I mention that the more you coach, the more your confidence will build?

The power of reflective learning

When I first started using coaching skills as a leader, I was given some great advice: keep a learning journal. I had an A5 spiral bound notebook in which I would debrief my coaching interactions. I considered a coaching situation from that day, and jotted down my thoughts on these three things:

- What did I do well in this interaction? Need to keep doing this, and perhaps do more.

- What did I not do so well? Opportunity to improve on that next time.

- What's the stretch for next time? Focus on pushing my boundaries.

Writing in, and reviewing, that journal gave me confidence, both in the 'doing well' reflection, and in the observation of my growth over time.

Confidence: Questions for the *leader who asks*

1. *Remember back to you when you first learned to ride a bicycle. Were you immediately confident? What was needed to build your confidence over time?*

2. *Think about a new skill you have learned recently. How well were you able to apply that skill the first time? What did you do to build confidence in that skill?*

3. *If you truly believed that failure was part of the learning process, how would you apply your coaching skills today?*

4. *What undermines your confidence? What could you do today to move past that block?*

5. *From which other areas of your life can you transfer confidence into your coaching skills?*

Courage

A coaching approach isn't for the faint hearted—the *leader who asks* needs courage.

We all carry 'stuff'. (That's a technical term for the multiple things that people create that get in their own way.) Your stuff might include beliefs you have about yourself, stereotypes you hold about leadership, scars from earlier hurts, fears about the future etc. It takes courage to consider your own stuff, and then to put it aside and focus on another person.

People are complex. Most of those people are not like us, and there's no user guide. It takes courage to work in the complexity and mess of others, as you need to do to become a *leader who asks.*

It takes a strong heart to care and connect deeply. It takes courage not to have the answers, and yet ask the questions anyway. For many leaders, it takes courage to ask rather than tell, to abdicate from the 'leader with all the answers' role.

Courage is not the absence of fear. In fact, the only time you will ever feel a complete lack of fear is when you are dead, or dead drunk. Neither are useful states for leadership. Courage is pushing through despite the fear, using the fear as data. Fearing less.

Josie shows courage

Josie was well briefed on staffing issues when she took over the new Project Management role. Christopher, the lead Business Analyst, had been 'a problem' for years and no one new how to deal with him. From what Josie could see, he had been left to his own devices, and others worked around his problematic behaviour, where possible mitigating the damage he was doing to client relationships.

Two weeks after she took on the role, Josie was clear on three things. The first was that she could not allow Christopher's behaviour to continue, and the second was that he seemed unhappy in his role. The third thing Josie knew was that she was afraid of how Christopher would respond if she attempted to tackle the issue. It was very tempting just to let his behaviour go, in the way that the two Project Managers before her had done.

Josie knew that as the leader who asks she needed courage, and she set up a time to talk with Christopher. Taking a coaching approach, and complementing her courage with curiosity and compassion, Josie was not surprised to learn that Christopher knew his performance was substandard. Her questions led to an open and honest conversation that uncovered that Christopher was bored and needed a new challenge.

Josie was able to coach him to a commitment on improved focus in the short term, and in the longer term to support him to find a new role elsewhere so that he could apply a broader subset of his skills in a new environment.

People want feedback

As I work with leaders and leadership teams, I often see a lack of courage in the area of providing feedback and addressing poor performance. The concerns leaders hold about providing 'constructive feedback' is often unjustified. People actually want the bad news that you don't want to give them.

Research has found that people want corrective feedback more than praise, providing it's given in a constructive manner. 72% of respondents said their performance would improve if their manager provided corrective feedback.[20] So be courageous and have the conversations that need to be had.

Emotional contagion

We all understand the concept of contagious germs. You cough on me, I 'catch' your cold. Do you know about the concept of 'emotional contagion'? It's just as it sounds: I can 'catch' your emotions.[21] It's important to note that the leader's level of emotional contagion is greater than individual team members. (Remember when I said 'your state matters'?)

The *leader who asks* is aware of emotional contagion, and is able to regulate their own emotional state for the benefit of their team. The coaching leader uses courage as an antidote for fear—not to suppress the fear, but simply to notice it, take heed of its message, and move through it to commitment and action.

Anna experiences emotional contagion

Anna was excited to be presenting to the board on the new strategy she and her team had been focused on for the last six months. She was well prepared and felt calm as she waited outside the boardroom. Calm until her CEO arrived. Anxious about whether Anna was ready and fearful about the board's reaction, the CEO radiated negative energy.

Anna felt her positivity slipping and her body tensing up. This is emotional contagion in action. The CEO was unaware of her own 'emotional wake', unable to recognise, label and regulate her emotions, instead letting her fear impact and limit her team.

Courage: Questions for the *leader who asks*

1. What might stop you from being courageous in your conversations with others? How could you let that go?

2. What do you believe about leadership and courage? How helpful are those beliefs?

3. What would be possible if you knew that by you role modelling courageous leadership, you empowered others to do the same?

4. When do you notice fear as you work with others? What is the fear telling you? What opportunity does the fear bring/mask?

5. What commitment could you make that will move you through the fear?

6. *What meaning do you give to courage? To fear? How would a strong commitment support that?*

7. *Think about a time when someone gave you 'constructive criticism' well. And another time when you were given critical feedback poorly. What can you learn from that?*

8. *What might others gain if you were willing to provide more feedback?*

9. *What conversation are you putting off having due to fear?*

10. *Think back to a time when the mood in your work team was good. Then 'that person' arrived— you know that person who is always sour and brings the group down. What did you notice about your emotional state? What about the emotional state of others? What can you learn from that?*

11. *How well do you regulate your emotional wake?*

12. *What conversation would you have this week if you had more courage?*

13. *Who would gain by you being more courageous in your conversations? And who else?*

14. *Thinking about a particular scenario in which you lack courage: What's the worse thing that could happen? How likely is that to happen? What could you do to minimise the likelihood and then proceed anyway.*

15. *What feedback are you holding on to due to a concern about the impact? What is the risk of continuing to hold onto this?*

Chapter 9

LEADER STATE:
About them

Rapport

Rapport is the key to building relationships. People like people who are like them. (Have you got that? People like people who are like them.) And one way to be liked by someone is to have rapport with them. When people feel a connection with you, conversations that are more meaningful and deeper relationships are possible. Distance and disconnect results from attempting to build a relationship without rapport.

So what is rapport? Rapport is being in a close or harmonious relationship with another person or group, where in that moment you understand one another's feelings or ideas and feel heard. It is possible (and even likely) that you will move in and out of rapport over the course of an extended discussion.

Think about a recent time when you were in conversation with someone where ideas and energy were flowing. Perhaps you felt so in tune that you didn't notice the time pass. If you had taken the time to notice, you probably would have found you and the other person were holding your bodies in similar ways, both leaning forward, or both with chin propped on one elbow, matching or mirroring one another's posture. This is an expression of rapport.

Research into the relationship between professional coach and client clearly demonstrates the importance of rapport in coaching relationships. 92% of respondents in the International Coaching Federation's 2012 global study indicated that the personal rapport between coach and client is very important.[22] While this refers to professional coaches in formal coaching situations, the *leader who asks* also needs to build rapport to have impactful conversations.

So while the *leader who asks* does not need to be liked, they do need to focus on building rapport. Warm feelings shown non-

Rapport is the key to building relationships.

verbally through voice tone and facial expression help. Daniel Goleman (psychologist and prolific writer who popularised the concepts of Social and Emotional Intelligence) maintains that positive feelings towards the other person (and vice versa) contribute to building rapport.[23]

Taking the time and focus to build comfort in people by communicating in their communication preferences, and to ensure that they feel 'heard' will support you in building rapport. *The Bible* tells us to 'do unto others as you would have them do unto you'. While this may be an excellent way of living, it is not an excellent way of communicating. To maximise the effectiveness of our communication, we need to 'do unto others as they would be done unto'. So, if I am calm and measured as a communicator, you will be most effective in building rapport with me if you can also be calm and measured. If I am strongly analytical, your arguments will be more persuasive if you are more analytical when speaking with me.

Michael struggles with rapport

Michael is a technical specialist whose advice is listened to by government and whose knowledge is respected internationally. He leads a statewide team, and while his team respect him, they struggle to make personal connections with him, many describing him as 'distant', 'aloof' and 'uncaring'.

In fact, Michael cares a lot about his people. He had the self-awareness to recognise his inability to build rapport and the limiting impact this was having on his leadership, but he did not know what was going wrong, nor how to fix it.

In working with me, we focused on his ability to recognise when to be analytical and technical, and when to focus more on people and emotions. This 'simple' strategy alone allowed Michael to build greater rapport with both his team, and non-technical external stakeholders.

Many coaching books have 'building rapport' as one of the most critical skills to master. While I accept the importance of this as a key competency for the coaching leader, I believe that if you demonstrate other coaching competencies covered here (especially listening, curiosity and compassion), rapport will result.

Three ways to build rapport in communication:

1) Match and mirror body language. Matching is where you adopt the same body language as the other person. Mirroring is where you are adopting 'opposite' positions. For example, as you face someone, they have their legs crossed right on left, and you will have your legs crossed left on right. Doing this overtly can be a bit 'icky' (no, that's not a technical term); instead, it's much better to avoid overt differences in body positioning that break rapport. So if they are learning forward into the conversation, avoid leaning back for example. Just let the matching and mirroring happen naturally.

2) Match voice pace and tone. This one is effective, and worth paying attention too. I am naturally an energetic and expressive communicator; my face is very expressive, I use a wide range of voice tones, and I employ lots of gestures, and at times speak very quickly. I am very conscious to match the voice pace and tone of less expressive communicators when I work with them, otherwise my communication mannerisms will get in the way of building rapport and negatively impact my ability to influence.

3) Match language. Words are, at best, an approximate indicator of the concepts we aim to communicate. As we discussed above in *Listening*, use their language in order to build and remain in rapport. If they talk about being 'rattled', you talk about being 'rattled', and not being 'uncomfortable', even if the two words mean the same thing to you.

And when (because it is 'when' and not 'if') you realise you are out of rapport with a person or group, that's okay, rebuild rapport before continuing.

So why does being in rapport matter so much? The coaching leader asks questions, and questions without rapport feel like an inquisition. The coaching leader is challenging, and a challenge without rapport feels like an attack. With rapport, we have connection. Without rapport, we have distance.

Rapport: Questions for the *leader who asks*

1. *Think about someone whose conversation challenges you in a productive way. What does that person do to maintain rapport despite the challenge?*

2. *Next time you are engrossed in a conversation with someone, take a moment to ask yourself 'what do I notice about the relative body language of both of us?'*

3. *What are some of the triggers that cause you to loose rapport?*

4. *What could you do today to build greater rapport in a meeting?*

Whatever you direct
your awareness to, you
will get more of that.

5. *How could you play with matching voice, pace, and tone to build rapport today?*

6. *What are your current strategies for building rapport? What will you add to that after reading this section?*

7. *On a scale of 1–5, how well do you tune into, and utilise, the language of others? What could you do today to move that score up one point?*

Focus

You get what you focus on. Whatever you direct your awareness to, you will get more of that.

Think about the last time you bought a car. Perhaps you made the decision to buy a silver Mazda 3, and then everywhere you look there are silver Mazda 3s. Surely, everyone must have decided to buy the same car as you and at the same time. Actually, it's just that you are filtering for Mazda 3s. They are relevant to you right now, and so that focus of relevance means your awareness is tuned in.

The science behind this is simple. Your Reticular Activating System (RAS) is a set of connected nuclei in the brain that filters incoming information to discriminate irrelevant background stimuli. By thinking Mazda 3, you have primed your RAS to filter Mazda 3s into your conscious awareness.

This happens at work too. When you believe someone is undermining the team, or can't be trusted, your awareness will be raised, and you will find abundant evidence that this is the 'truth'. This is known as the 'Golem Effect' where people will perform to the low standards you expect of them, and it's unhelpful.[24]

The opposite happens too. In the 1960s, there was a (now) famous study done at the Spruce Elementary School in San Francisco. Kids were given a false IQ test, and the teachers were told that randomly assigned kids had potential. What's remarkable about this study is that over the next year, those kids excelled. In fact, by the end of the year, their IQs had risen by up to 29 points.[25]

Were the kids any different at the start of the year? No! The assignment of potential was random. What was not random was the way the teachers related to these kids, the expectations they had of them and, therefore, what they focused on.

So when we expect a person to rise to a new challenge, and we support them to do so, they will. As the *leader who asks*, I am sure you can see that the Pygmalion effect is more useful in building individual performance and team culture, than the Golem effect. But how do we see the best in people? We focus on the intention, and not on the behaviour.

Behaviour verses intention

Behaviour is an external expression of all that is going on for a person internally. Their behaviour is what we see, hear and experience. Intention is internal, and another person's intention is often not clear to us.

Behaviour that seems unproductive on the surface, regardless of how it looks, largely comes from a positive intention. As the *leader who asks*, your challenge is to hold that belief when faced with undesirable behaviours at work, because what you focus on will determine what you get.

This is not to say that you become Pollyanna, tripping over your rose coloured glasses, as you believe the best in people despite evidence to the contrary. This is about focusing on intention—

getting curious, asking questions, showing compassion: all competencies we are soon to address.

When you are able to work with someone to identify their intention, their awareness is developed and new opportunities are created.

People are looking at your behaviour without knowing your intention

We judge ourselves by our inside intentions; the problem is that others judge us by our outside behaviours. They take our behaviours and put them through their own translation system to determine what they 'know' to be our intention.

For example, if we were inside their head we would hear internal dialogue like 'If I were being that provocative in a discussion, it would be because I was intending to create division between the two teams. That is what this person's behaviour feels like to me; therefore, their intention is to create division.'

Think back to a time when you thought you were communicating one thing, but the people around you heard something completely different. It's happened to all of us. Perhaps you were in a meeting when you were enthusiastically contributing, and yet others judged you as taking over? Or maybe it was the opposite. You were considering your ideas carefully before speaking, and you couldn't get a word in. Others may have thought you were withholding ideas, or even sitting and silently judging them.

For the *leader who asks*, the challenge is to be overt with your intentions, and work to align your behaviour with your intentions.

Be overt with your
intentions, and work
to align your behaviour
with your intentions.

Developing Direct Reports: Taking the guesswork out of leading leaders is the last book I wrote with my co-authors Anneli Blundell and Belinda Cohen. It centres on the theme of behaviour verses intention, and outlines behaviour and intention of the 12 most common leadership derailers. It's a great read (even if I do say so myself!) if you are interested in better understanding leadership behaviour and intention.

Camillo is overly directive

Camillo leads a specialist team of engineers. When we look at his behaviour, it's easy to see him as untrusting and overly directive, regularly finding fault in the work of his people. Camillo's behaviour has led to workplace tension, even complaints lodged against him.

When we understand his intention, it's easier to understand his behaviour. Camillo is driven by a strong commitment to the community, and his vision of housing for everyone drives all that he does. Camillo has very high standards and so sets the bar high for himself and his team.

Taking a traditional approach, a leader may send Camillo on a leadership training program, or counsel him to wind down his directive approach, encourage him to delegate more. In fact, this had been tried with Camillo unsuccessfully in the past.

The leader who asks would help Camillo to build awareness about how his behaviours and intentions are perceived by others, as the first step to developing more leadership flexibility.

Focus: Questions for the *leader who asks*

1. *How can you better align your behaviour with your intention?*

2. *Thinking about a recent situation that didn't go so well, how could you have better aligned your behaviour with your intention?*

3. *When have you felt misunderstood at work, because other people misinterpreted your actions? If you were coaching yourself, what questions might you ask to help you better align your behaviour and intention?*

4. *What will support your inquiry into the intention of others before judging their behaviour?*

5. *What behaviour are you noticing? What intention are you ascribing to that behaviour? What other intentions might this person have?*

6. *If we work on the basis that all behaviours have a positive intention, what positive intentions might this person be expressing now?*

7. *Thinking about someone whose behaviour puzzled you this week: what interpretations of their possible intentions can you come up with?*

8. *Thinking about this week, where have you focused on someone's behaviour, when a shift to their intention would have served them (and you) better?*

9. *What are the key risks for you as the leader who asks, in focusing on behaviour at the expense of intention?*

Curiosity

Curiosity creates relationships. It brings people together—it doesn't kill cats. A mindset of curiosity is vital for the *leader who asks* because it creates an openness that allows true exploration.

As leaders, when we judge people, they feel it. They may not be sure how or why they feel uncomfortable; they will know that there is some sort of barrier between you. Judgment limits our growth, cripples relationships, denies us possibilities and keeps us small.

Curiosity is the antidote for judgement. Like a spritz to the face on a hot day that wakes us up, curiosity refreshes our relationships and our perspectives. That's what we need in business (and in pleasure!).

The *leader who asks* is curious. Leaders like AG Lafley, chairman and CEO of Proctor and Gamble who, each week, asks himself 'What am I going to be curious about?' He does this to remind himself that the strategic insight needed from a CEO requires deep curiosity.[26] Curiosity is needed by leaders at all levels of the organisation.

Ari was lacking curiosity

Ari considered himself a people-person, and working in HR that's a good thing. He has a good life; he is committed to his family and passionate about his work. Yet there are always people in his life thwarting his intentions for happiness and success—'those people' who get in the way. (You know the ones—perhaps you have some in your life too?)

When I suggested to him one day, 'Ari do you think you're judgmental in the way you see people?' He responded, 'no! But there are just some people who are terrible at their jobs'.

And then he softened, opening to the possibility that the constant judgments he was making about people were creating tension for him and getting in the way of his relationships.

He agreed to my challenge to send me a daily text for two weeks, telling me about a judgment when he noticed he had made one and was able to let it go.

Texts arrived for two days as promised, and on the third day this email:

> I found myself judging a truck driver this morning on the way to work again for not driving the way I felt that he 'should' – eg the way I would have done it. I then found myself again judging people all day: the woman who talked about her twins, the manager not managing his team properly, the woman who left documents in the photocopier, the homeless guy at the front of our office.
>
> All of a sudden I realised it's not them, it's me.

Ari wasn't curious. He was judgmental, and his judgments were blocking any real relationships or connections happening. He was disempowering the people he was working with, when his intention was to develop them.

His judgments about himself—constantly not meeting up to his own expectations—were also exhausting him. This lack of awareness had come at a high personal and professional cost.

Becoming consciously aware of these judgments has been Ari's first step; the second step was letting them go. After only two weeks, this had a significant positive impact on his tension levels, his happiness, his relationships, and his ability to coach others.

When you find yourself getting frustrated with someone you are coaching, ask yourself what judgments are you making about them, the situation, and/or about yourself in relationship to them. Try curiosity instead.

Get curious about what might be driving their behaviour, what outcome they are seeking, their choice of strategies, what barrier they need to overcome to move forward, and why you feel the way you do about this?

Curiosity: Questions for the *leader who asks*

1. *What judgements have you made about others today? How well are they serving you and the people around you? What do you need to do to let them go?*

2. *Make a list of five judgements you have made in the last week about others, and get curious. How would you know if this was really true? What if it weren't? What other judgements might be possible? What other judgements could someone else make? Embrace the openness that follows this.*

3. *Where could curiosity about your own motivations help you support others?*

4. *Where are you stuck in your views on a work situation or person? What is that about? How might someone else view that? And another person? Get curious about the different perspectives that might be possible, and what each might do for you.*

5. *How do you feel when you are judged? How does feeling judged impact your desire/ability/motivation to do a good job?*

6. *Think about a recent time you felt judged by someone else? What made you feel judged? What could the other person have done to help you feel less judged? What can you learn from that?*

7. *What could help you move from judgement to curiosity about this particular person or situation?*

8. *What do you need to believe about yourself to be open and curious?*

9. *What do you need to believe about the other person to be open and curious?*

10. *What judgements are you making about the other person/situation/prospect of success that might be limiting your potential and theirs?*

Chapter 10

LEADER STATE:
About the space

Questions

Questions trump directions. In fact, I would go so far as to say that the question mark is the golden child of punctuation.

When you give directions, the person's 'rational brain' may be listening, but this won't necessary help with recall or ownership. Nor will it help someone apply the 'advice' you have just given them to other contexts.

As we mentioned in Chapter 3 (How does the *leader who asks* support insight?), questions are more likely to lead to self-discovery, insight and the results you want.

Stop telling. Start asking.

Voltaire had it right, when a long time ago he said, 'Judge a man by his questions rather than his answers.' Clearly, he was much wiser than Ronald Reagan who, famously said, 'Before I refuse to take your questions, I have an opening statement.'

The March–April 2017 Harvard Business Review features an excellent article *Bursting the CEO Bubble: Why executives should talk less and ask more questions.*[27] The hypothesis of the article is that the CEO's greatest responsibility is to recognise when a major change in direction is needed. Yet the power and privilege of being a CEO can leave you insulated from information that might allow you to detect the need for change. The antidote for this is to ask more questions.

Elon Musk founder and CEO of Tesla and SpaceX says 'A lot of times the question is harder than the answer'.[28] If you can properly phrase the question, then the answer is the easy part.

Ask:Tell ratio

Here's a simple way to build your awareness around questions. Monitor a conversation you have with someone who reports to you. Notice your 'Ask:Tell ratio'.

How often are you asking searching questions that cause them to think and lead them to their own answers? And how often are you telling them what to do? What more could be possible if you upped the percentage of ask?

And how about your team meetings? How often are you in broadcast mode, spouting forth the latest updates and parroting key corporate messages? How often are you asking them questions that challenge people to think, and encourage them to relate corporate messages to their own work and life?

The next time you lead a team meeting, monitor your Ask:Tell ratio.

Steven asks more questions

Steven was a mid-level manager in the financial services sector. While he has always been passionate about his work, after this recent promotion, he was leading a much bigger team, which was geographically dispersed, and he felt overwhelmed. Needing to do everything and have all the answers for his team was becoming a burden. His frustration levels were rising, as his team members seemed to lack the initiative to sort things out for themselves.

Steven moved to a coaching approach, primarily by tracking his Ask:Tell ratio. This was initially confronting when he realised that he 'told' most of the time and rarely 'asked'. As he became more thoughtful, pausing before responding, and asking more questions, Steven noticed the initiative levels of the managers reporting to him picked up. His own workload progressively decreased, after initially increasing, when he noticed that at first asking questions took longer than giving solutions.

The final evidence for this being a valuable approach was the annual performance reviews. He was more relaxed than he had ever been, the conversations flowed, and two of his direct reports said they were the best performance conversations they had ever had.

All questions are not created equal

There are two types of questions: stupid questions and sensible questions. Only kidding. While there may be 'no such thing as a stupid question', there are types of questions better suited to different situations.

Broadly speaking, there are two types of questions:

1. Open questions are just that. They open up the conversation and there are multiple possible answers: 'what would you like to achieve by tomorrow?'

2. Closed questions typically have a yes/no or single word answer: 'can you do that by tomorrow?'

Open questions

Open questions are best used when you want to gather ideas and open up possibilities. Open questions lead to expansive thinking, shifting and dissolving boundaries, and opening new lines of enquiry.

Think of the classic question words that create open questions:

- Who?
- What ?
- When?
- Where?
- Which?

Did you notice there is one 'w question' missing from that list? 'Why?' is missing. What's the reason for this do you think?

Imagine I asked you, 'Why did you do that?' (You might also be imagining me with my hands on my hips and using an accusatory tone.) If you were successful in imaging that, what did you notice about your immediate response? 'Why' should be avoided as it can lead to defensiveness and shutting down—not the response you want in a coaching conversation.

As an experienced coach now, I use 'why' sometimes with my clients. I use it infrequently and advisedly, and only when I have a solid rapport with the client, in both an absolute sense and in that specific moment. Before I reached this level of mastery, even as a professional coach, I avoided 'why?'

That's a shame right, as *why*? is useful. I can hear you thinking, 'Without *why*, how can we find stuff out and guide people around us to find stuff out?' We can ask other things instead. Try these alternatives:

	Why?	=>	Alternative questions
1	Why did you do that?	=>	I am curious as to your thinking on that one.
2	Why do you want 'x'?	=>	What is it about 'x' that is so important/attractive to you?
3	Why did 'x' upset you?	=>	Talk me through what was going on for you in relation to 'x'.
4	Why do you care so much about that?	=>	Help me to understand what's behind that for you.
5	Why would you take that direction?	=>	Tell me more about your thinking on that direction.

Closed questions

Closed questions narrow thinking and shut down possibilities, and should be avoided when you want to generate ideas, and build expansiveness and creativity into the coaching conversation.

Closed questions should be used when all options have been identified, and it's time to get specific, or when you are testing and confirming commitment. Closed questions can also be used effectively to confirm understanding.

1. Are you ready to commit to that?

2. Is this achievable by 1 March?

3. Of the three options you have just outlined, which one would you like to take forward?

4. What time will you call me on Friday to tell me this is complete?

Be cautious of non-questions in sheep's clothing

When I teach leaders coaching skills, I regularly see them struggle to ask truly open questions. Often we ask closed questions weakly disguised as open, 'So do you think you should confront Fred with this performance issue?' is a closed question. As is, 'Are you going to confront Fred or are you going to ask your line manager to do it?' Both questions narrow down options; they are questions that demand a yes/no answer.

You could ask 'How might you approach Fred with this performance issue?' and if you are near the beginning of the conversation, 'What could you do to address this performance issue?' would be even more open.

The other risk is an assertion thinly disguised as a question. Hiding your telling by putting your solution in a question is not a real question. 'Hmmm … That's a difficult one. Perhaps you could discuss that with the Nick in advance? How do you think that would work for you?' is not really question—it's an embedded suggestion. Nor is 'Do you think you would like to talk to Nick's boss about that?' a real question.

When you give the answer within a question, it's not really a question.

But they just want the answers: Back-to-you questions

If you and the people around you are new to a coaching approach, everyone needs to learn the new game, and you will probably find yourself in situations where they just want you to give them the solution. A few fabulous questions will save you, and keep the responsibility for thinking on them.

If the coachee continually wants you to tell them what to do, consider asking one of these back-to-you questions:

- What do you think I am going to advise you to do?
- What is the next question I need to ask you right now?
- What is the question you don't want me to ask you right now?

The final two questions below really work. They may seem a little weird until you have used them a few times and have experienced for yourself how they get good results:

- If you did know the answer, what would it be?
- Let's imagine that we had changed roles. Imagine I have just come to you and said <repeat their story using their words>. What would you tell me to do next?

The first one takes the conscious mind off guard, and the unconscious mind usually steps forward to answer. And the second question relies on a perspective shift—the problem is no longer theirs, it's yours. I can guarantee they will have an answer for 'your problem'.

When you **do** need to tell them

There are times, as a leader, where you do need to 'tell'. Support your people to integrate and apply the information you have given them, and encourage them to make their own connections with questions such as:

1. How might this work here?
2. What surprised you about this?
3. What would you do differently to what I have just outlined?
4. What similar experiences have you had in the past?

5. How can we leverage this to have the biggest impact?

Questions: Questions for the *leader who asks*

1. *What's your Ask:Tell ratio now? What opportunity does that highlight?*

2. *What beliefs do you hold about leaders needing to provide answers? How might those beliefs be impacting your leadership approach?*

3. *Which leaders do you know that ask good questions? What can you learn from watching them?*

4. *What situation can you try out more questions in?*

5. *Thinking about the last few meetings that you led, what opportunities did you miss for asking questions? If you can turn back time, what questions could you bring into that conversation?*

6. *How can you ask questions that guide understanding and lead them to draw their own (relevant) conclusions?*

Uncertainty

It's okay not to have all the answers. This is an especially important one for a new leader. Nobody expects that you will know everything. In fact, your team want to be involved in getting to the truth and creating the answers.

The *leader who asks* needs a willingness to play with uncertainty. They are curious and draw wisdom from their team. In doing so, they empower others to contribute, which results in shared accountability for the outcome. The truth is often unclear at best and ambiguous at worst. Vulnerability and the willingness to not know is essential. Conversely, arrogance is dangerous (and often inaccurate).

As leaders, we understand about uncertainty, right? Sure, we won't always have all the answers. But what does uncertainty mean in relation to coaching? When you take a coaching approach, you won't always know where the conversation is going. And occasionally, even after you have had the conversation, you won't know where it has been. Yes, I know that sounds odd.

Corrinne in the hot seat

When I trained as a coach, there was a 'hot seat' activity. A student was selected to sit in the 'hot seat': the 'fire' under the chair—sticks and flames of red and orange cellophane—was quite realistic. From the hot seat, we coached someone else, while the rest of the group watched.

When it was my turn, I coached Jacinta, who had a very different personal and professional background to me. This showed in the different language we used to explain situations and express ourselves. Being at the front of the class, I was especially conscious of doing the 'right' things— asking questions, using her language, attentively listening.

During much of this 25-minute coaching conversation, I was lost and uncertain exactly what we were talking about. I held the space, stayed calm and kept going. At the end of the conversation, Jacinta was inspired and had a much greater degree of clarity. She found our conversation very helpful, even though I was not sure what we were talking about.

The *leader who asks* is able to recognise and work with a level of uncertainty for themselves, and to support others through their uncertainty.

'Keep Calm and Carry On' was a motivational poster produced by the British government in 1939. It was one in a series of posters in preparation for the Second World War. The poster was intended to raise the morale of the British public and keep them focused when threatened with the predicted mass air attacks.[29] 'Keep Calm and Carry On' is just what you need to do when faced with the uncertainty of the direction or specific content of a coaching conversation.

What do the brain scientists tell us?

A fundamental organising principle of the brain is to move towards reward and away from threat. Certainty is perceived as rewarding to the brain, and when we have certainty, it's possible to measure increased activation in the reward neural circuitry of the brain. [30] Experiments have shown that dopamine (a hormone associated with the reward circuitry) neurons in monkeys fire during the expectation of a reward, and also in the expectation of information about that reward.

Conversely, increased uncertainty increases activation in the threat neural circuitry and decreases activation in reward circuits. Personality traits can also impact the way people process and respond to uncertainty, and will determine how much uncertainty is needed to trigger a threat response.

The *leader who asks* is able to recognise and work with a level of uncertainty for themselves, and to support others through their uncertainty.

It's important to keep in mind that the coachee is likely to also be feeling a level of uncertainty, and be experiencing a level of threat response. Coaching is about change, and change often involves ambiguous feelings: both wanting and not wanting things to change are part of the process. Allowing your coachee to express these inner conflicts and avoiding pushing towards a solution before they are ready, will enable you to be a better listener. (In other words, match the pace of your coachee by accepting the ambiguity and delaying your own need for closure.)

Ways to reduce the threat response of uncertainty

- Accept that uncertainty can generate a threat response—it's normal—'Keep calm and carry on'.

- Draw confidence from having been able to work through uncertainty in the past.

- Remember your role is supporting them to work though the situation; this does not require answers (or certainty) from you.

- Focus on what you know *is* certain, to reduce levels of anxiety for you and the coaches.

- Use their language. That will help them gain clarity, and you don't need full understanding of what their words mean to coach effectively.

Uncertainty: Questions for the *leader who asks*

1. *What certainty do you have? (Keep that top of mind.)*

2. *What is driving your need for certainty? How can you relax the grip that need has on you?*

3. *Consider the last time you faced an uncertain coaching conversation: what can you learn from that?*

4. *What personal qualities could you bring into this conversation to be comfortable with ambiguity that may be present in a conversation?*

5. *Where else in your life can you practise relaxing your need for certainty, so that you can bring this skill into the coaching space?*

6. *What do you need to do or believe to give yourself permission not to know?*

7. *How might you frame a coaching conversation to reduce the level of uncertainty experienced by the coachee?*

Empathy

The energy you bring to every conversation creates the tone. When you show up with compassion, understanding is possible and indifference is not. Your role, as the *leader who asks*, is to hold the space so breakthrough and insight can happen. Your care-factor matters.

Henry shows another way is possible

Early in my career, I met a man who demonstrated that an entirely new level of empathy and compassion was possible in business, and that showing this level of empathy enabled tough conversations without confrontation or hurt.

Henry and I were working with a dynamic CEO, Nathan, who possessed a fragile ego. I watched and listened in awe as Henry gave Nathan some truly honest feedback that I wasn't sure Nathan was willing or able to hear. Henry's care factor was high. It was obvious that his comments were offered from a place of service and empathy for Nathan and the situation.

His words were clear, and because the feedback was offered in support and development of Nathan (and not about Henry), his words were heard and absorbed. In that interchange, Henry set a standard of empathy to which I have aspired ever since.

Empathy is sometimes confused with sympathy, so let's clarify the difference, as sympathy is not helpful in coaching.

Empathy is defined as 'the power of understanding and imaginatively entering into another person's feelings'.[31] Sympathy is 'the fact or power of sharing the feelings of another, especially in sorrow or trouble; fellow feeling, compassion, or commiseration'.[32] So empathy is about UNDERSTANDING the feelings of another, sympathy is about SHARING those feelings.

While there is a place for both processes, in leadership empathy is more useful and less taxing on your energy. As leaders, we want to be able to understand the emotions (and probable emotions) of others and to have the skill to demonstrate our understanding. We don't necessarily want to share the feelings. Understanding gives us insight with an appropriate detachment, whereas sharing emotions could render us less able to assist.

Through empathy, Henry was able to understand and connect to Nathan, and then offer his observations with compassion—that's a skill needed by the *leader who asks*.

Empathy will impact your whole team

Building empathy will also impact the success of your team. Research conducted by MIT looked at characteristics that distinguished smarter teams from the rest and found that it wasn't the IQ of the individual team members that made the difference. Even more interestingly, teams with members who were more motivated to contribute to their group's success were not more successful.[33]

One of the three factors that made the difference was social sensitivity: the ability to read complex emotional states that were measured via a test for empathy.

Paul Elkman best known for his work studying facial expressions and emotion, has classified three types of empathy[34]:

- **Cognitive empathy**. Perspective-taking: knowing how the other person feels and what they might be thinking.

- **Emotional empathy.** Emotional contagion: feeling physically as the other person does and being well-attuned to another person's inner emotional world.

- **Compassionate empathy.** People with compassionate empathy not only understand a person's predicament and feel it with them, but are spontaneously moved to help, if needed.

The *leader who asks* displays all three types of empathy to better understand themselves and the people they lead.

Empathy: Questions for the *leader who asks*

1. Thinking about what you are about to say: is it for you or for them? Learning or punishment? Building or bruising? Check in on your empathy level.

2. If your energy had a flavour, what flavour would it be right now? How well will that serve you and/or the

person you are working with? What flavour would take you to understanding faster?

3. On a scale of 1–5, what level of empathy do you feel for the person you are working with? What would move that up?

4. On a scale of 1–5, what level of empathy do you feel for yourself in this situation? What would move that up? And what reduces your empathy for yourself?

5. If you wanted to increase your level of indifference in this situation, what would you need to do/think/ believe/feel? And what would the opposite of that achieve?

6. What could you do today to develop empathy for your peers, and extend that empathy into your relationships?

7. What is getting in the way of you being empathetic? What needs to happen to move past that?

Chapter 11

LEADER STATE:
About the relationship

Grounded

This chapter could be described as the 'fine print'. It underlines and undermines everything I have said to date. Good cooks use a recipe to get ideas, and then with an understanding of the ingredients, they relax into the recipe—they 'forget' it even—and enjoy cooking the food. The *leader who asks* can take the same approach.

So what does being grounded mean in this context? It's about being fully present with the person/people with whom you are talking. It's observing what's going on for them and for you, and being comfortable with that. It's feeling okay in the moment so that you are able to respond to whatever comes. Forget the process—get grounded! Being grounded allows you to be responsive to the energy and the needs in the moment. Dance an agile dance rather than follow a fixed process.

When I was four, my mother gave me a blow up Play School punching clown. I remember playing with it in the sunshine on the back veranda of our house. It was teardrop-shaped, as tall as me, and had a big red nose. It had water in its flat base, so that no matter how hard I punched him in the nose, he would bounce up again. This groundedness came from the heavy base, giving my smiling clown resilience no matter what. Being grounded in a coaching conversation is like having the solid base of the punching clown.

Of course, this is easier said than done. Any new skill takes time to develop, and is likely to feel clunky at first. The more skill and confidence you develop in all the core competencies for a coaching leader, the more grounded you will be in coaching conversations.

Grounded: Questions for the *leader who asks*

1. On a scale of 1–10, how grounded do you feel in your current coaching conversations? For any score above 1/10, what has contributed to that? How could you raise the score further?

2. What things might happen in a coaching conversation that would throw you off balance? What could you do to relax your responses to those things?

3. If there were one of these other eleven core competencies that would contribute the most to being grounded in the coaching conversation, what would that be? How could you build that skill over the coming month?

4. What is distracting you in your coaching conversations? What reminder(s) might help you stay present?

5. What expectations are you placing on yourself in this conversation that put you under pressure?

6. What mindset preparation do you need to do before the conversation?

7. How can you shape your coaching space (environment) to remove distractions such as your computer or phone?

Purpose

'Why did you set your alarm this morning?' That was the question the aerobics instructor asked us at 6:00 am. Were we there to tick the 'exercise' box? Or were we there to really make a difference to our health and wellbeing? Good question! I upped my pace, as I was definitely there to make a difference to my health and fitness after Christmas and four weeks of holiday indulgence! Her question was a good reminder of my purpose.

The *leader who asks* has a clear purpose for their conversations, and facilitates discussion towards that direction. Having a purpose gives form, and provides a direction towards an outcome, preventing pointless wandering. The *leader who asks* ensures their conversations have purpose, whether this is one on one while waiting for the photocopier, in semi-formal fortnightly catch-ups with a direct report, or in a team meeting.

In pure coaching with a professional coach, the purpose of the coaching conversation comes entirely from the coachee. The *leader who asks* often exercises more influence than that, co-creating the conversational purpose with the coachee.

What are some broad types of purposes you could have in taking a coaching approach? These might include building awareness, developing new behaviours, extending skills, correcting poor behaviour, developing new competencies, problem solving, generating new ideas, leading a team meeting or bringing a group of people together around a common cause.

Regardless of the occasion in which we are using coaching skills, we need to know why we are having a conversation. Questions are the best way to clarify the purpose:

1.   Do you want to run an effective meeting? Use coaching skills. Where do you want to get to by the end of the meeting?

2.   Are you running a sales conversation? Use coaching skills. What outcome are you seeking? What outcome would make this a good use of your time?

What outcome would make this a good use of your (potential) client's time?

3. Are you responding to a problem from a team member? Use coaching skills. What outcome is being sought?

4. Are you holding a performance conversation? Use coaching skills. What direction do you want to maintain? What behaviours do we want to shift?

I hate shopping for clothes. When I head to the shopping centre on my own, I can spend hours wandering and leave frustrated having purchased nothing. So I have a secret weapon—a personal stylist—Nicole Vine. She keeps me focused. When I shop with her, we shop with purpose, which we agree on in advance. Then Nicole has a plan mapped out, and she is constantly checking in with me. We focus on the outcome of the trip, and we actually come away with a new wardrobe that works. Nicole helps me develop a clearly articulated purpose, and then she holds us both to that purpose, making sure there is no aimless wandering.

A key thing to remember here is that the coachee must have ownership of and commitment to the conversational purpose, or outcomes are unlikely to be achieved. When the *leader who asks* is progressing their own agenda without consideration of the coachee, agreements may not be honoured and gaols unfulfilled.

Natalie runs effective meetings

Natalie had an 'ah-ha' moment in a Leader Who Asks training program. She could run meetings that are more effective and achieve better outcomes by being very clear on purpose. She realised that in her organisation, meetings were a big part of the culture, and yet very few were useful.

Now, she never attends a meeting without being very clear on the overarching purpose of the meeting, and what she specifically wants to achieve from the discussion. She begins all meetings with a discussion that ensures there is a shared purpose among meeting participants. That clarity allows her to guide the direction of the discussion, and with the buy-in of the group, keep everyone focused on the main objectives.

Purpose: Questions for the *leader who asks*

1. *What outcome do you want from this conversation?*

2. *What outcome does the coachee want?*

3. *When do you set the agenda, and when would the coachee set the agenda? What difference could that make?*

4. *What domains of your leadership have unhelpful purposeless conversations? What will you do to resolve that?*

5. *How could you bring a more focused purpose into your meetings?*

6. *Thinking about a recent meeting you attended that was chaired by someone else, how clear and shared was the purpose? What did the chair do/miss that increased or reduced clarity of purpose?*

7. *What purpose do you have in initiating this conversation? What is the purpose for the coachee? How might this differ if you or the coachee initiates the conversation?*

8. *How best can you align the outcome you want with the outcome they want?*

9. *What outcome does the task/team/organisation want to achieve?*

10. *How will you know this outcome has been achieved?*

11. *What will success look like?*

12. *If this was a really effective conversation, what will have shifted by the end?*

13. *What direction would have the biggest positive impact?*

14. *Why does this outcome matter?*

15. *What will prevent you from wandering in this conversation?*

16. *Who do you need to be to support your coachee to achieve this purpose?*

Belief

Belief creates opportunity. When you believe an alternative future is possible, growth is enabled. Belief (followed by action) thwarts stagnation.

Before May 6 1952, there was a universal belief that it was not possible for a human being to run a mile in under four minutes. Many had tried and proved it could not be done. On 6 May 1952, Roger Bannister ran a mile in 3 minutes 59.4 seconds. His record lasted only 46 days. Was there a shift in training technique over the two months? Or massive improvement in running shoes or diet? No—Bannister's achievement shifted belief. Once he did it, others 'believed' a sub four-minute mile was possible. And then they found it was.

Your beliefs and
expectations can serve
to expand or contract
a person's potential.

In Chapter 6 we discussed the Pygmalion effect, the psychological principal that describes people's propensity to live up to the high expectations you hold of them. When translated to leadership, this can create a form of self-fulfilling prophecy for those we lead.[35]

Belief is an important tool for the *leader who asks*. Your beliefs and expectations can serve to expand or contract a person's potential. In my own mentoring work, I will often say to a client whose lack of self belief is preventing them from achieving a milestone: 'I will hold the belief for you while you do the work'.

Fixed and growth mindset

Stanford Professor Carol Dweck has conducted and interpreted ground-breaking research into what she has termed 'fixed' and 'growth' mindsets.[36] She describes these as two ways of thinking and viewing yourself and the world:

Fixed mindset is the belief that skills, talents, and capabilities are predetermined, finite and, therefore, cannot be developed. You either have a talent, or you don't, and the same applies to other people.

Growth mindset is the belief that talents and abilities can be developed over time; that there is a potential to foster new skills in yourself and others.

The *leader who asks* has a growth mindset, and believes that people can and will over time get better at what they do through learning and experience. They see failure as an opportunity that could lead to mastery, and take full responsibility for their own learning.

In contrast, leaders with a fixed mindset experience an urgency to prove themselves. They avoid situations with a high likelihood of failure because success depends upon protecting their fixed qualities and concealing their deficiencies. When failure does occur, the focus is on rationalising the failure rather than learning from it.

What is your prevailing mindset?

These mindsets apply to how you think about yourself, and how you think about (and develop) others. They shape how you respond to the world. Adopting a growth mindset and believing that skills, talents and capabilities can be cultivated and developed will not only support your coaching approach, it will also fast-track your own growth and potential.

As Dweck says, 'Mindsets are just beliefs. They're powerful beliefs, but they're just something on your mind, and you can change your mind.'

Jasmin can't coach

Jasmin has a fixed mindset and believes that her ability is predefined. She is genuinely surprised that she has reached a senior leadership role, despite her self-diagnosed lack of ability. Jasmin is one of the very few people I have not been able to support to develop coaching skills, because she refused to believe this leadership approach was possible for her, and that she had the ability to learn. She was not wiling to risk 'failure' through a messy application of newfound skills. Jasmin retained her command and control leadership style, and missed the opportunity to approach leadership more lightly.

Belief: Questions for the *leader who asks*

1. What beliefs are you holding about your own coaching capability that may be limiting your ability to coach others?

2. Where has a lack of belief limited your ability to achieve something in the past? What did you learn from that situation that you could usefully apply to coaching?

3. Thinking about a particular person you wish to support with a coaching approach, what positive beliefs do you hold about them? What limiting beliefs do you hold? What are the implications of both (think Pygmalion and Golem effects)?

4. Where have you worked with someone in the past, whose ability you underestimated? What can you do to avoid that in future?

5. When you think about your own coaching ability, is your approach more towards a fixed mindset or a growth mindset? How could you develop more of a growth mindset?

How you show up matters

The *leader who asks* is conscious of how they show up, including the energy they bring into the conversation, the way they impact others, the coaching 'space' they create and the relationships they build.

We have covered 12 key competencies and you will already be skilled in some of these. Which competencies, when further developed, will make the biggest impact on your leadership? Focus on building those first.

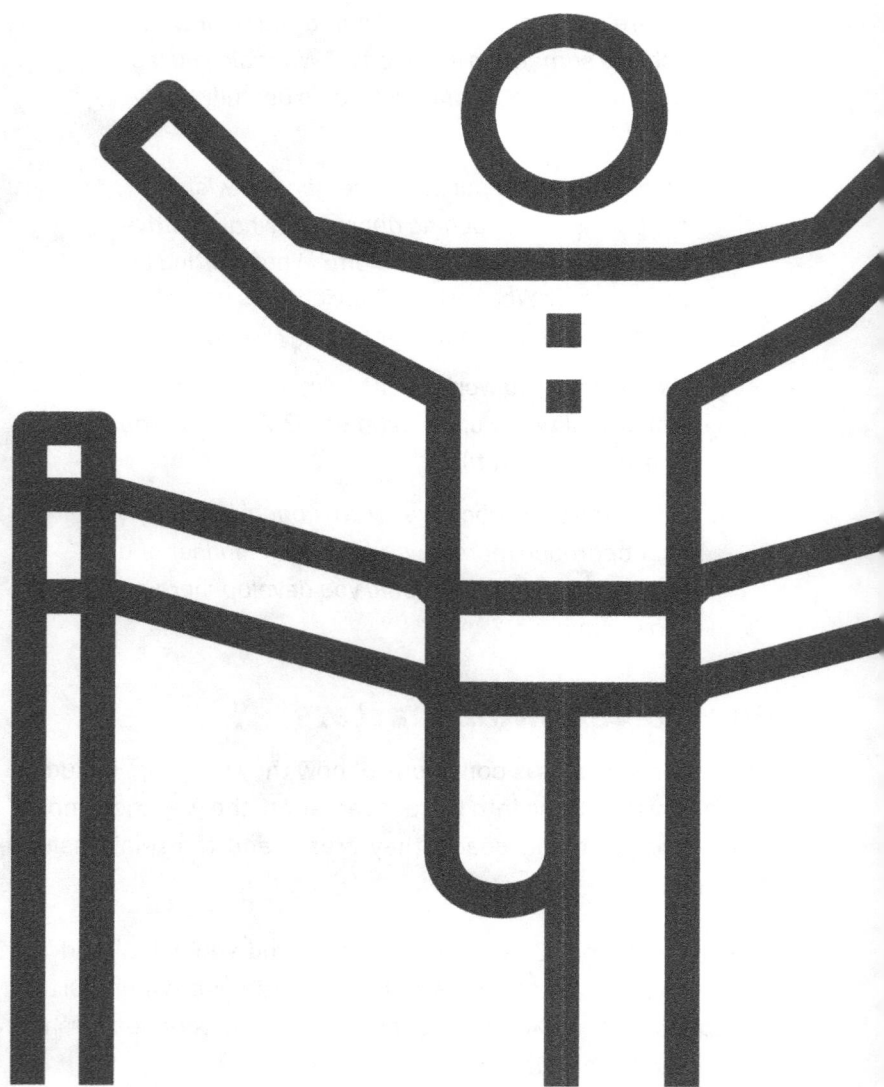

Chapter 12

The *Leader Who Asks* in action

When to coach: Situational leadership

Having coaching competencies in your leadership toolkit offers major advantages. Knowing when to use those competences—and when not to—provides the edge.

Corrinne misjudges a coaching moment

Many years ago, when I first learned coaching skills, I was excited with my new abilities to help people through sticking points, and delighted with the results I was getting. After a week or so, my husband was telling me about a problem that he was experiencing at work, and I moved into full coaching mode. It wasn't a pretty outcome! I realised too late that this was not a coaching moment, and have been much more careful ever since.

As we said at the beginning, the best leaders are flexible in their approach. Situational leadership was developed by Ken Blanchard and Paul Hersey, and is explained in Blanchard's *Leadership and the One Minute Manager*.[37] Blanchard outlines four basic leadership styles and the importance of using each adaptively to suit the needs of the individual and the situation.

I think about situational leadership as having the flexibility to choose your leadership style based on the people, the task and the situation in the moment. In other words, not every scenario is a coaching moment.

The *leader who asks* chooses when, how, why and with whom to use their coaching capabilities.

The *leader who asks* chooses when, how, why and with whom to use their coaching capabilities.

The full end-to-end coaching framework can be followed when there is a coachee who needs assistance to resolve a challenge or change a behaviour. This might include formal or semi-formal coaching conversations during annual performance reviews, career guidance conversations, regular one:one meetings, performance management discussions, project start-ups, project debriefs, etc.

There is a time and place for complete coaching conversations. And there's a greater, and more practical need for 'corridor conversations' that stretch and grow people, and build cultures. Short, spontaneous and impactful conversations can happen anytime, anywhere.

The competencies of coaching can be used **almost all the time** in conjunction with the leadership style you judge to best suit the moment. In fact, these are the competencies of good leadership. In this chapter, we will delve into examples of the *leader who asks* in action through a number of common leadership scenarios, and explore the key core competencies used in each.

The *leader who asks* runs effective meetings

Core competencies: Purpose, Questions, Uncertainty

Have you ever been to a bad meeting? Most of us have. Perhaps it is a poor use of your time because:

a.   The agenda was unclear, meaning the wrong people were there?

b.   The conversation lacked focus and purpose?

c.   The meeting host/chair talked **at** you?

    d.   Communication flow was all one way?

    e.   All of the above?

How many hours a day do people at your work spend in meetings? How long do they spend preparing? I am guessing your answer ... and it's not pretty, right?

And how effective are those meetings in:

    a.   communicating key messages?

    b.   formulating plans, generating ideas, and developing insight?

    c.   engaging people?

Many leaders run unfocused and boring meetings that lack a clear purpose and lead to few actionable agreements.

Thomas changes his approach

Thomas spent too long preparing for meetings, primarily driven by the need to be in control and the misguided belief that, as the leader, he needed to have all the answers.

Learning coaching skills challenged his sense of identity as a leader, helping him to see that his role was guiding, supporting and developing his people, and ensuring that together the team developed the answers. He needed to curate the answers, and not know them.

Coaching skills also gave him a new approach to running meetings. He got clear on the purpose to provide direction,

Short, spontaneous
and impactful
conversations can
happen anytime,
anywhere.

ask questions, listen curiously and carefully to the answers, and hold true during any uncertainty.

His meetings become lighter, more productive, people contributed, and best of all, Thomas spent a lot less time preparing a choreographed approach.

So how does the *leader who asks* use coaching competencies to run meetings that get outcomes and that people want to attend? They approach the meeting with a coaching lens that will include things such as:

- Being clear on their intention before they call the meeting.
- Issuing an agenda with a clear purpose.
- Using questions throughout the discussion to clarify issues, gain acceptance and secure accountability for future actions.
- Communicating outcomes, agreements and next steps at the end of the meeting.

The *leader who asks* self-coaches

Core competencies: Purpose, Focus, Curiosity

Sometimes I find myself getting stuck. In my case, it's typically because I can see too many options, and then I get confused and can't find the way out. Usually I am able to coach myself to a solution, sometimes following the 3D model end-to-end, and sometimes just by applying some of the coaching competencies.

I usually start by asking myself what am I trying to achieve. This helps me build awareness around my purpose. Sometimes this is enough. Being clear on the outcome I am trying to achieve sometimes helps the way forward become obvious.

I also ask myself what I am focusing on. Is it behaviour or intention, both mine and that of other people? Focusing on curiosity as a way into my thinking and being open to what I find is important. I know that if I begin to judge myself it will start a downhill spiral.

When I am **really** stuck, I ask someone else to coach me. Do you have a coach? A powerful way to support your own development is to find a coaching buddy—a peer who both coaches you and seeks coaching support from you.

The *leader who asks* inducts a new recruit

Core competencies: Questions, Listening, Belief

It's very easy to view inducting a new member of your team as a 'training' opportunity. You show. You tell. They do. (And hopefully they remember when you walk away.)

The *leader who asks* uses more ask and less tell wherever possible to help a new recruit learn all that is needed. Not only will asking questions that prompt them to generate their own solutions increase the likelihood they will remember, it will also help them apply knowledge from previous roles to this one.

Of course, there will be some things you need to 'tell'—back to situational leadership. What does the person, the situation and the task need right now? Listening is also a critical skill in inducting a new team member. New people bring a fresh perspective, and can make observations and ask questions that lead to insight for the coaching leader.

A new recruit may not know what questions to ask. The coaching leader can ask questions to find out what is most important for the new recruit to feel accepted and confident in the role. How's your belief in your new recruit? Remember the Pygmalion effect (where your belief will lift their performance) and the Golem effect (where your lack of belief will reduce their performance). The *leader who asks* creates opportunity for growth by believing in their people, and then supporting them to fulfil expectations.

The *leader who asks* at a networking function

Core competencies: Questions, Confidence, Curiosity

Many leaders—especially introverted leaders—confess to disliking 'networking events', and yet they are a part of professional life in many sectors. Your coaching competencies can help you get through a breakfast gathering for all staff, as well as a cocktail party product launch for clients.

The *leader who asks* has a couple of open questions that will help begin conversations with people they know and with complete strangers. Here are a few you might want to try:

1. What has been the highlight of your last week/month/quarter?

2. What has been your journey to get here today?

3. What are you hoping you will gain from the guest speaker's presentation?

4. What did you enjoy about the guest speakers presentation?

5. How would you address the challenges outlined by the speaker?

6. Where would you be tonight if you weren't here?

7. What are you interested in outside <topic of the event>?

Having an approach to begin a conversation will give you confidence and faith that you can get through the event, and even enjoy it and have some interesting conversations.

Allowing your natural curiosity to shine through will help you engage others with less effort. Get curious about them. What's their world view? What's been the journey that's led them to do the work they do? What do they enjoy about it? If they didn't need to work, what would they like to do instead? People enjoy talking to someone who is genuinely interested in them.

The *leader who asks* meets a client

Core competencies: Rapport, Purpose, Listening

When the *leader who asks* meets a client, building rapport is at the top of their mind. A relationship can be built when a connection is made.

We are all busy, and time is a resource to be treated with respect. Being clear, up front, on the purpose of a meeting will ensure that their time and yours is wisely invested. Upfront questions like, *what do we each want to gain from this meeting* or *what do we want to have achieved by the time we part today?* allows the purpose to be mutually agreed.

Real listening gives you a presence in the conversation. People feel heard, and you are more likely to gain insights that will facilitate a deeper connection. Remember the 3 Golden Rules of Listening for the *leader who asks* 1) 80-20 talk time, 2) use their language and 3) allow the silence.

The *leader who asks*
takes every opportunity
to connect with people.

The *leader who asks* in the lunchroom

Core competencies: Questions, Belief, Courage

In the lunchroom, by the water cooler, waiting for the lift ... the *leader who asks* takes every opportunity to connect with people. Growth opportunities are not limited to formal development conversations or six-monthly performance reviews. Corridor conversations are possible throughout the day.

As Susan Scott, author of *Fierce Conversations* says,

> Our work, our relationships, and our lives succeed or fail one conversation at a time. While no single conversation transforms a company, a relationship, or a life, any single conversation can. Speak and listen as if this is the most important conversation you will ever have with this person. It could be. Participate as if it matters. It does.[38]

Brendan focuses questions to increase his corridor coaching

*Brendan and I were working on increasing his adoption of coaching skills, knowing that this was the key to allowing him to release some of the operational load and focus on more strategic work. Starting in **discovery**, Brendan self-assessed his use of a coaching approach, and especially his use of questions, as:*

- *Formal coaching opportunities (bi-monthly Capability Planning one:one conversations). 'Doing well.' —4/5*

- *Informal (100 questions that get fired at me during the day).'I answer automatically and then 60 seconds later realise I have done it.' —1/5*

- *Informal (catch-ups that I initiate such as project status check-ins). 'I start with questions and end up giving answers.' —3/5*

*So he knew how to 'ask' and not tell, and he was confident in coaching. So why wasn't he doing that all the time? Hmmm ... time for **decoding**. For Brendan, the formal conversations worked well because he thought about them in advance, and actively moved into a coaching mindset. It was the requests and questions he fielded during the day where he went straight into telling. Probing why that was so, the three key factors he identified were 'habit', 'time' and 'the desire to help'.*

When we explored that further, Brendan was clear that while in the short term it took less time to answer the question than to coach the people to their own solution, in the long term he was maintaining a dependency on him, which was soaking up his time. He also had a significant insight in his desire to help. He was actually 'helping too hard', and denying his people developmental opportunities on the job.

*Brendan **developed** a pathway forward to break his telling habit and lead to a more conscious response when his team members fired questions at him.*

For the next three weeks, he would ask one question (and then possibly more) before giving an answer. To get started, he would choose two of the questions below, which we developed to keep top of mind each day and reviewed after three weeks:

1. *What have you done so far? What were you planning to do next?*

2. *What do you recommend?*

3. *What's the difference between <one option> and <another option>?*

4. *What are the implications of <what they have asked about>?*

5. *What do you think I will suggest you do?*

6. *What have you seen work in the past in this situation?*

(We tested five of the '100 questions' he had had that day and found that all of these questions would work with each scenario.)

Brendan's approach was successful, and within a few months, he found he had more time in his day to be strategic and his people were working more independently.

Assuming that your people have the answers they need takes belief. When the *leader who asks* shows faith in them, growth is more likely. When you mindlessly provide the answers, skills stagnate. Of course, if you have someone who is doing something for the first time, perhaps they don't have all the answers they need just yet, and you may need to 'tell' as well to help them grow.

It takes courage to try a new approach. Remember Paul, the Committed Leader we met in Chapter 2? His sense of identity as a leader was as a 'fix it man', and it took courage to step away from constantly providing solutions. If he wasn't constantly providing the answers, was he really needed? Paul's commitment to becoming the *leader who asks* gave him the courage to stop giving the answers.

The *leader who asks* in a performance conversation

Core competencies: Questions, Compassion, Focus

Most leaders dread annual performance review time, and often they are put off so long that the frustration levels are very high.

Think back to a recent time when you needed to have a performance conversation with a team member. Perhaps they weren't meeting their key result areas. Or perhaps their behaviour was out of line with organisational culture. Where was your focus? Was it on the behaviour the team member had been exhibiting, or on their intention?

Lois shifts her focus

Lois was frustrated with Mitch's performance. Mitch was a gifted analyst, and he led a technically brilliant team. Mitch's constant delaying tactics were driving Lois mad. He seemed reluctant to make a decision, and his clients were complaining to Lois that waiting for him was creating bottlenecks in projects. Lois's own experience was that they would agree on a way forward, and then Mitch would not take action, becoming defensive with her when she asked for a status update a few days later. Despite her frustration, Lois committed to shifting her focus from Mitch's behaviour (delaying, over-researching, not making decisions) to his intention by using the 3D model.

Discover

Lois began the performance conversation by asking Mitch how he believed his performance was tracking. Listening carefully, she guided Mitch's attention to two of the current projects he was leading.

Her questions helped Mitch identify the concerns of his clients and realise that from their point of view, there was a problem. He gained insight, for the first time, that his continual focus on conducting more research was impacting others negatively and had the potential to damage his professional credibility.

The compassionate way she conducted the conversation meant that Mitch felt safe enough to be open; they developed a shared understanding of the problem and its impact. They agreed that the goal was for Mitch to make timely decisions so that projects were not derailed and that his key stakeholders felt confident with his professional expertise.

Decode

With that goal in mind, Lois was able to shift her focus from Mitch's behaviour (delaying, over-researching, not making decisions) to his intention. Her questions guided Mitch to understand the motivations behind his own behaviour. The cause of his 'delaying' was the very good intention of wanting the 'right' decision. But in a fast moving technology space, 'right' was unlikely. Mitch realised that making the 'best decision possible with what he knew in the moment' was critical. Without Lois's support to help him become aware of this underlying motivation, and reframing that, it would have been very difficult for Mitch to achieve his goal of making timely decisions.

> **Design**
> *Together Mitch and Lois developed a plan to help Mitch a) remain mindful of making the 'best decision possible in the moment' and b) make timely decisions. The plan included how Lois could support Mitch, and how they would track shifting perceptions from Mitch's clients.*

The *leader who asks* has an awareness on both the behaviour and the intention driving that behaviour.

The *leader who asks* develops others

Core competencies: Rapport, Questions, Confidence

A colleague gave me some great informal coaching years ago. She asked me how I thought another peer had just experienced feedback I had offered him. Her question got me thinking, and I asked her how she had experienced that same feedback. Her reply: 'The feedback was insightful but it was delivered with a sting. How could you deliver that same feedback without the sting?'

I still remember that very clearly, and 'feedback without sting' is a mantra I consciously remind myself of from time to time. Clearly, three minutes of micro coaching had an impact on me, and she was only able to do that because she had built rapport with me. In that moment, there was a relationship between us and I felt a connection. She cared enough about me to challenge me, to ask.

She also had confidence in herself and faith that she could hold that conversation.

When good asking goes bad

Sometimes leaders try a coaching approach for a short time, and then give up. Here are the top six reasons why a coaching approach fails, and what to do about it.

1. Too much telling, too little asking

We have talked about the implications of telling: people tune out, forget what you say, fail to accept accountability, disengage etc. Telling denies our people the opportunity to learn for themselves. After reading a book called '*Leaders Who Ask*', it's hard to imagine this happening, right? And just in case it does, here's what to do.

Mitigations:

- Monitor your Ask:Tell ratio.

- Ask a question before 'telling' anything.

- Begin with a few questions, and gradually build your repertoire.

2. You followed the framework and forgot your state

A beautiful coaching framework (such as the 3D model) perfectly executed by a leader focused on judgement, or a leader not listening, will never result in a beautiful coaching conversation. The framework is a helpful guide. Focus <u>first</u> on your state as a leader; otherwise, your questions may feel more like integration than a supportive conversation.

Mitigations:

- Go back to the Core Competencies mapped out at the start of Chapter 7. How are you showing up? Where do you need to focus?

- Remember that these seven Core Competencies
  are the most important (and the others will come
  with time and practice): Listening, Courage, Focus,
  Curiosity, Questions, Compassion and Purpose.

3. You focused on *your* agenda and not *coachee's* agenda

Yes, you are the leader. And right from the start of this book I
said that you have more influence over the direction of the
conversation than a traditional coach might. And ... if it's only your
agenda that's getting your attention, it's likely to feel like telling,
regardless of the number of question marks in your grammar.

Mitigations:

- Ensure that the purpose of a conversation is co-
  created and agreed up front, and that the coachee
  has input into outcomes. (Core Competency: Purpose)
- Recommit to listening and review the Listening Core
  Competency.

4. Lack of clear outcome and accountability

Asking and not telling does not imply a lack of accountability. One
strength of a coaching approach is a mutually agreed purpose that
gives the conversation direction. An accountability framework
should be agreed in the **design** phase of a coaching conversation.
Due to the nature of coaching, a coachee should feel a strong
sense of accountability to delivering the results agreed.

Mitigations:

- Review your last few coaching conversations. Was a
  clear purpose agreed? If not, focus on ensuring that
  happens in your next coaching conversation.

Becoming the *leader who asks* and building your coaching competencies, takes time, focus and practice.

- What about accountability? Did the coachee commit to actions that are measurable? Was an accountability framework put in place? If not, that's an area for future focus.

- Were you invested in the outcome, and not the coachee? Look out for that next time.

5. It wasn't really a coaching opportunity

To a carpenter with a hammer, everything looks like a nail. Not every moment is a coaching opportunity. Just as 'telling' in every situation is unwise, the same goes for asking. Sometimes swift and decisive action is needed by the leader. At other times, you might be guiding someone who does not have the knowledge or experience to answer the questions, and another approach such as mentoring would be best.

Mitigations:

- Make a conscious choice in the moment about whether this is a coaching opportunity, based on what is best for the people, the situation and the task.

6. A coaching approach felt awkward, so I gave up

Becoming the *leader who asks* and building your coaching competencies, takes time, focus and practice. You can expect to feel awkward. Interestingly, people in my Leader Who Asks training programs often report feeling uncomfortable and having 'clunky' conversations when I give them practice time. Yet the person being coached reports the conversation as 'natural' and 'in flow'.

You know what's needed to get past each of these failure points. Give it a go. See what happens. Practice makes perfect.

Chapter 13

Developing the business case for a coaching approach

When you are considering a division or organisational-wide strategy for developing a coaching approach, you might want to look into the broad areas listed here to better quantify the cost of doing nothing and the potential benefits of a coaching approach.

Costs of doing nothing

It may seem easier to stay as you are, and to retain your existing leadership style and cultural profile. But there are costs of not stepping up and becoming the *leader who asks*.

- Absenteeism: Direct cost of sick leave and indirect costs of wider impact.

- Presenteeism: Indirect cost of staff being at work and not engaged.

- Workplace conflict: Direct cost of bringing in expertise to resolve conflicts. Indirect costs of reduced productivity, leader's time, and impact on team morale.

- Staff turnover: Loss of expertise, impact on productivity, impact on customer relationships, direct and indirect recruitment costs, time to skill up new hire.

- Unmet Key Performance Indicators: These will vary by individual and team function.

- Customer service: Direct and indirect costs associated with poor customer service and customer complaints and attrition.

- Reputational impact (in extreme cases).

There are costs
of not stepping up
and becoming the
leader who asks.

Benefits of a coaching approach

The benefits of a coaching approach that lead to a Fearless Culture are also diverse.

Tangible benefits

- Increased engagement (staff engagement surveys, organisational pulse check surveys)
- Productivity: individuals and teams meeting KPIs
- Increased retention/decreased staff turnover
- Reduced absenteeism
- Customer satisfaction: customer satisfaction surveys and anecdotal feedback
- Shift in culture survey results (for organisations moving towards a target culture and tracking results).

Intangible benefits

- Leaders focused less on operational issues and day-to-day reactive problem solving, and more on strategic and value adding activity
- Changed nature of exit interview commentary when staff leave
- Qualitative feedback from across the organisation, which may include 360 feedback
- Leaders and staff feeling they have been invested in as leaders take a coaching approach to offering regular on-job development
- Preferred employer status

- Delivering on brand promise.

Of course, each situation will be different, and my clients measure Return on Investment in different ways depending on the organisation, the current situation, and the intended outcomes.

Are you ready to build a Fearless Culture?

Leaders with coaching skills in their leadership toolkit can build a Fearless Culture. Research undertaken by Bersin by Deloitte found that organisations where senior leaders 'very frequently' coached had 21% higher business results. This research also stressed the importance of providing skills to leaders. Organisations within their sample that were highly effective at teaching managers to prepare for the coaching relationship were approximately 130% more likely to have strong business results.[39]

Fearless Cultures are developed by leaders throughout the organisation. They bring out the best in their people through conversations—formally and informally—every day.

Are you ready to develop **leaders who ask** and build a Fearless Culture?

A final word

My daughter and I took up roller blading (she was aged seven and I was closer to 50 than 10!). When we started, I spent more time on my knees and backside than I did on my wheels. (In fact being fully transparent, I bruised places I didn't think it was possible to bruise, and my husband accused me of being an irresponsible parent by putting my own safety at risk.)

Start slowly, notice
the results you get,
celebrate your learning.
Practice. Go lightly.

Gradually, with practice, I improved. My aspirational goal was to zoom confidently along the beach bike path. I'm not there yet, and I know that practice will take me closer to that goal.

So as you develop your coaching muscle, remember it's a progressive development. Start slowly, notice the results you get, celebrate your learning. Practice. Go lightly.

The rewards are there for the *leader who asks*.

Corrinne's profile

Corrinne incites people to play their big game through Fearless Leadership.

As a well-recognised instigator of change and growth, she empowers leaders to realise the potential in their careers, teams and organisations. Corrinne draws on over 15 years' experience in the corporate world heading large teams and projects with budgets in excess of $80 million. She knows firsthand the practicalities of juggling multiple priorities and perspectives.

In addition to a science degree and postgraduate business qualifications are her impressive accomplishments as a registered project manager with the Australian Institute of Project Management, an accredited Master Certified Coach with the International Coaching Federation, and a certified Neuro-Linguistic Programming (NLP) Practitioner.

Some of Corrinne's greatest wisdom (and best stories) come from living and working in a jungle refugee camp at the edge of a war zone where she gained powerful insights into leadership and an active passion to help others avoid its pitfalls. Married to an ex-freedom fighter and mother of two daughters, she appreciates the importance of balance in a team.

Corrinne is a dynamic speaker and influencer. A leader of leaders, she is well-versed in leadership theory with a natural ability to inspire and equip others to uplift and unite the most dysfunctional of teams. She has trained over a thousand leaders across a broad scope of backgrounds and challenges them to build engaged, productive teams.

Honest, empathic and results-focused, Corrinne helps you leverage your team's diversity and collective brilliance to establish an edge that distinguishes you from your competitors. Her Fearless Leadership framework is innovative and trusted, informed by positive psychology and underpinned by Neuroscience.

Renowned names attesting to the success of her approach include Bendigo Bank, Bank Australia, Royal Children's Hospital, Metropolitan Fire Brigade, Worksafe, Dulux Group, NAB, GE Healthcare, Griffith and Monash Universities, and numerous local councils.

Corrinne is co-author of *Developing Direct Reports: Taking the Guesswork Out of Leading Leaders* (2015) and *Cracking the Code for Workshop Performance* (2014).

Get in touch

To find out more about working with Corrinne, contact Corrinne's Relationship Manager:

Phone   03 9576 8437
Email   hello@corrinnearmour.com

Connect with Corrinne:

Twitter   @corrinnearmour
LinkedIn   http://au.linkedin.com/in/CorrinneArmour
Mail   PO Box 6029 Booran Road, Caulfield South 3162, AUSTRALIA
Web   www.CorrinneArmour.com

Endnotes

1. Deloitte, 2012. The leadership premium: How companies win the confidence of investors. March, p. 5.

2. James, C., 2014. *The Sydney Morning Herald*. [Online]
Available at: https://www.smh.com.au/business/small-business/how-to-manage-a-micro-manager-20131211-2z5cx.html [Accessed 12 June 2018].

3. Dale Carnegie Research Institute, 2012. *Dale Carnegie*. [Online]
Available at: https://www.dalecarnegie.com/en/resources/emotional-drivers-of-employee-engagement
[Accessed 12 June 2018].

4. Gallup, 2013. State of the global workplace: Employee engagement insights for business leaders worldwide. p. 78.

5. Ashdown, N. & Leow, M., 2014. *Bring out their best: Inspiring a coaching culture in your workplace*. s.l.:Palmer Higgs Books Online.

6. Whitmore, J., 2002. *Coaching for performance: Growing human potential and purpose - the principles and practice of coaching and leadership (People skills for professionals)*. s.l.:Nicholas Brealey Publishing.

7. Blakey, J. & Day, I., 2012. *Challenging coaching: Going beyond traditional coaching to face the facts*. s.l.:Nicholas Brealey International.

8. Davachi, D. L., Kiefer, D. T., Rock, D. D. & Rock, L., 2010. Learning that lasts through the ages. *NeuroLeadership Journal*.

9. Davis, J., Chesebrough, C., Rock, D. & Cox, C., 2016. Why insight matters. *NeuroLeadership Journal*, September, p. 6.

10. Davis, J., Chesebrough, C., Rock, D. & Cox, C., 2016. Why insight matters. *NeuroLeadership Journal*, September, p. 5.

11. Davis, J., Chesebrough, C., Rock, D. & Cox, C., 2016. Why insight matters. *NeuroLeadership Journal*, September, p. 6.

12. Davis, J., Chesebrough, C., Rock, D. & Cox, C., 2016. Why insight matters. *NeuroLeadership Journal*, September, p. 7.

13. Symons, R., 2015. *Red Symons Breakfast Show.* [Sound Recording](ABC Radio Melbourne). [Accessed 14 April 2015].

14. McGregor, J., 2015. The head of the Gates Foundation on combatting 'CEO disease'. *The Washington Post*, 21 December.

15. Bryant, A., 2015. Sue Desmond-Hellman: Helping people find their sweet spot. *The New York Times*, 25 April.

16. U.S. Department of Labor, 1991. *Skills and New Economy.* Washington, DC: U.S Government Printing Office.

17. Trimboli, O., 2017. *Deep listening: Impact beyond words.* s.l.:Oscar Trimboli.

18. Kanter, R. M., 2014. Overcome the eight barriers of confidence. *Harvard Business Review*, 3 January.

19. Kay, K. & Shipman, C., 2014. *The confidence code: The science and art of self-assurance - what women whould know.* s.l.:HarperBusiness.

20. Zenger, J. & Folkman, J., 2014. Your employees want the negative feedback you hate to give. *Harvard Business Review*, 15 January.

21. Barsade, S., 2014. *Faster than a speeding text: Emotional contagion at work.* [Online]
Available at: https://www.psychologytoday.com/blog/the-science-work/201410/faster-speeding-text-emotional-contagion-work [Accessed 16 June 2018].

22. International Coaching Federation, 2012. *2012 Global Coaching Study: Final Report*, s.l.: s.n.

23. Coleman, D., 2016. *Leaders: Learn the art and science of rapport.* [Online] Available at: https://www.linkedin.com/pulse/leaders-learn-art-science-rapport-daniel-goleman/ [Accessed 16 June 2018].

24. Rosenthal, R. & Jacobson, L., 1968. *Pygmalion in the classroom.* First ed. New York: Holt, Rineheart & Winston.

25. Ellison, K., 2015. *Being honest about the pygmalion effect.* [Online] Available at: http://discovermagazine.com/2015/dec/14-great-expectations [Accessed 16 June 2018].
26. Gregerson, H., 2017. Bursting the CEO bubble. *Harvard Business Review*, Issue March-April, p. 83.
27. Gregerson, H., 2017. Bursting the CEO bubble. *Harvard Business Review*, Issue March-April, p. 77–83.
28. Gregerson, H., 2017. Bursting the CEO bubble. *Harvard Business Review*, Issue March-April, p. 78.
29. Wikipedia, 2018. *Keep calm and carry on.* [Online] Available at: https://en.wikipedia.org/wiki/Keep_Calm_and_Carry_On [Accessed 16 June 2018].
30. Rock, D. D. & Cox Ph.D, C., 2012. SCARF® in 2012: Updating the social neuroscienceof collaborating with others. *NeuroLeadership Journal*, Volume 4.
31. Dictionary.com, 2018. *Dictionary.com.* [Online] Available at: https://dictionary.com [Accessed 18 June 2018].
32. Dictionary.com, 2018. *Dictionary.com.* [Online] Available at: https://dictionary.com [Accessed 18 June 2018].
33. Wolley, A., Malone, T. W. & Charbis, C. F., 2015. Why some teams are smarter than others. *The New York Times*, 16 January.
34. Ekman, P., 2018. *Paul Ekman Group.* [Online] Available at: https://www.paulekman.com/ [Accessed 16 June 2018].
35. Rosenthal, R. & Jacobson, L., 1968. *Pygmalion in the classroom.* First ed. New York: Holt, Rineheart & Winston.
36. Dweck, C., 2007. *Mindset: The new psychology of success.* s.l.:Ballantine Books.
37. Blanchard, K., Zigarmi, P. & Zigarmi, D., 1986. *Leadership and the one minute manager.* s.l.:HarperCollins.
38. Scott, S., 2003. *Fierce conversations: Achieving success at work and in life, one conversation at a time.* New York: Piatkus Books Limited.
39. Bersin, n.d. *Deloitte.* [Online] [Accessed 28 February 2017].

www.ingramcontent.com/pod-product-compliance
Lightning Source LLC
Chambersburg PA
CBHW070714220326
41598CB00024BA/3141